LIVE FOODS LIVE BODIES!
RECIPES FOR LIFE

JAY & LINDA KORDICH

SQUAREONE
PUBLISHERS

Live Foods, Live Bodies! is not intended as medical advice. It is written solely for informational and educational purposes. Please consult a health professional should the need for one be indicated. Because there is always some risk involved, the author and publisher are not responsible for any adverse effects or consequences resulting from the use of any of the suggestions, preparations, or methods described in this book. The publisher does not advocate the use of any particular diet or health program, but believes the information presented in this book should be available to the public.

EDITORS: Joanne Abrams, Marie Caratozzolo, Colleen Day, and Michael Weatherhead
TYPESETTER: Gary A. Rosenberg • COVER DESIGNER: Jeannie Tudor

Square One Publishers
115 Herricks Road
Garden City Park, NY 11040
(516) 535-2010 • (877) 900-BOOK
www.SquareOnePublishers.com

Library of Congress Cataloging-in-Publication Data

Kordich, Jay.
 Live foods, live bodies! / Jay & Linda Kordich.
  pages cm
  ISBN 978-0-7570-0385-1
  1. Functional foods. 2. Nutrition. 3. Cooking. I. Kordich, Linda.
 II. Title.
  QP144.F85K67   2013
  612.3—dc23
                                                2012034162

Printed in the United States of America

10   9   8   7   6   5   4   3   2   1

Contents

PART THREE

Our Living Recipes

This book is lovingly dedicated to our sons,
John and Jayson,
who continually inspire us to share, teach,
and motivate others to live a long, disease-free, joyful life.

This book is also dedicated to you,
the reader,
who has the courage to transform yourself
into someone who feels eternally youthful and healthy.

Acknowledgments

We would like to thank to all of our friends at Facebook for the daily inspiration and love that they share with us.

We also thank the entire team from Live Foods, Live Bodies for helping us make our teaching beautiful, inspirational, and powerful. In particular, we acknowledge the help of Chika Machida, for her online support and content; Mike Conkle, for decades of dedication to the cause; Dan Riley, for his brilliance in creating magic on film; Martha Cesari, for her strong determination to keep the faith; and especially Rick Cesari, for his courageous commitment to Jay's mission of teaching the world to juice.

Lastly, we would like to thank Rudy Shur, president of Square One Publishers, for believing in our body of work and for bringing us the greatest executive editor, Joanne Abrams.

Introduction

The book that you are holding in your hands has the power to change your life. *Live Foods, Live Bodies!* is a truly revolutionary program that my wife, Linda, and I have practiced for a combined total of nearly one hundred years—sixty-four years of my life and thirty-two years of Linda's. Because we have dedicated our adult lives to achieving and promoting the highest standards of living health, you can be assured that Linda and I are experts in our field. *Live Foods, Live Bodies!*, which we have created together, offers solid guidance in attaining vital health and longevity. We invite you to hear our story and learn how you, too, can create a diet and lifestyle based on living foods, design your own "living" kitchen, boost your health and stamina, and give yourself—as well as your loved ones—a long, disease-free life. The greatest gift I can give this world before I leave it is an understanding of these priceless principles of living health.

"Our bodies are our gardens—our wills are our gardeners."

—WILLIAM SHAKESPEARE, PLAYWRIGHT

OUR STORY

You may remember me as the author of *The Power of Juicing,* which reached #1 on *The New York Times* Best Seller list in 1992. You may also have seen the infomercial for my juicer, in which I taught millions of Americans about the life-giving benefits of fresh juicing that I discovered shortly after being diagnosed with bladder cancer in 1948. Prior to then, I was like most people; I ate high-fat, high-sugar foods like meats, dairy products, junk food, and desserts, and paid little attention to my health. Cancer was my body's way of telling me that I had to shape up. Doctors told me that I had less than one year to live.

Luckily, I was young and open-minded. I instinctively turned to nature and decided to try holistic medicine. I was fortunate enough to find a well-known holistic cancer doctor from Germany, Dr. Max Gerson. He started me on a diet of living (raw) foods and juice that would change my life forever. Eventually, I added some pure organic foods and cooked soups back into my diet, but with a new awareness of how and when to eat them. I have been following this diet ever since.

Now ninety years young, I feel wonderful and more certain than ever in my beliefs about the benefits of living foods. It is my life's goal and passion to let others know that it is possible to wake up each morning feeling refreshed, vigorous, and alive; that it is possible to ward off fatigue and disease, and live a life full of stamina and vitality; and that it is never too late to regenerate your body. Sharing my personal story and making others aware of the key to lasting health—living foods—has remained important to me throughout the years. In 2001, my wife, Linda, and I made a serious commitment to spread our message about the positive power of living foods.

The success of our juicing message was actually due to the expertise of Linda, who is the strength behind all that I do. Linda became a vegetarian at only ten years of age, was juicing every day by the age of twelve, and was a proponent of juicing long before we met. While I was known as that "juice guy," Linda was a known expert in her own right as a teacher of vegetarianism and veganism, as well as a living foods advocate. Throughout our more than thirty years of marriage, she and I have enjoyed an empowering juicing and eating lifestyle. Together, we not only make a knowledgeable and experienced team, but also prepare deliciously satisfying foods and juices!

In addition, we spent three years creating a program based on our unique vegan living foods diet, which we pres-

"Nothing will benefit human health and increase the chances for survival of life on Earth as much as the evolution to a vegetarian diet."

—ALBERT EINSTEIN, PHYSICIST

ent to you in this book. Our quick and easy-to-follow system provides you with the understanding and motivation needed to develop a lifelong appreciation of living foods as the foundation of optimal health. Although juicing has been my personal savior and passion for over sixty years, I have also spent most of my entire adult life teaching about the power of living foods and plant food enzymes—the heart of our lifestyle program.

THE POWER OF LIVING FOODS

My core message has always been that *live foods build live bodies.* Living foods are powerful, whether in juice or food form. Your body needs living, fresh, colorful fruits and vegetables that are full of living *enzymes,* biological molecules that facilitate practically every chemical reaction that occurs in your body. They are the catalysts for energy and vitality, and the missing link to longevity and disease-free living. Live foods are also rich in a type of nutrient that I referred to as a "yet unidentified element of life and growth" before scientists introduced the term *phytonutrient.* Phytonutrients, or plant nutrients, are compounds that have been shown to offer life-sustaining benefits and disease-prevention properties. Enzymes and phytonutrients should be ingested every single day. This may seem like a daunting task, but just wait. You will soon see that it is not hard at all. This book provides you with all the tools necessary to make a living foods diet easy, convenient, and enjoyable.

One common misconception about vegetable juices and vegan foods is that they are tasteless and boring. The recipes and juice combinations that we use in our program prove this idea wrong. Some people once thought that carrot juice, for example, was strange and unappetizing. However, my Carrot and Apple Juice combination (see page 162) quickly changed their opinion. As you will learn, sometimes all it takes is flavorful dressings and spices or creative combinations to transform the taste of your food and change your old ways of thinking. The recipes presented in Part Three (see page 81) are so easy to prepare and delicious that you'll quickly leave behind your former eating habits without ever

"The food you eat can either be the safest and most powerful form of medicine or the slowest form of poison."

—ANN WIGMORE, HOLISTIC HEALTH PRACTITIONER

looking back. Included are some of the best healing recipes that Linda and I have been using for over thirty years, as well as recipes that the great Dr. Norman Walker and Dr. Max Gerson shared with me in 1948.

We also hope to help you recognize that buying health-oriented, life-force-enhancing kitchen tools and appliances, juicers included, is only the first step towards vital wellness. If they sit unused in your kitchen, they are of no benefit to you. Regular—and enthusiastic—use of these appliances comes from truly understanding how they enhance your health and quality of life. Inspiration combined with applied knowledge is the key to success in any venture.

YOUR LIFE CAN CHANGE—ARE YOU READY?

A living-foods diet will truly change your life. You wouldn't believe the stories we have heard about people who have adopted this lifestyle only to have their aches and pains, bowel and skin problems, and various health challenges disappear. They felt more alive and energetic than ever before, and this can be your story as well. You, too, can achieve optimal wellness, and live into your nineties with all your faculties intact.

As you embark on this new path of eating and living, you will learn the secrets to vital health that have sustained me for all of these years. One of these secrets is summed up in a question that I would like you to ask yourself every time you sit down to eat: *How much of my meal is alive?* This may seem strange, but you will understand the true meaning and importance of this question once you have read this book.

"It's the juice from the fiber that feeds you!"
—JAY KORDICH

Our advice is to take it slow and read each chapter carefully. Transition into your new lifestyle gradually, and don't beat yourself up if you make a few mistakes along the way. Remember, slow and steady wins the race. With *Live Foods, Live Bodies!*, you will gain an awareness and understanding of living foods that will transform the way you eat forever.

PART ONE

Understanding the Power of Living Foods

The living foods diet has been part of our lives and the lives of our children for a long time, but we know that—while it is wonderfully simple and natural—it is a new and unfamiliar concept to many people. Perhaps you are now wondering what a living foods diet can offer you. Part One was designed to explain exactly why and how this way of eating can positively transform your life and those of your loved ones, giving you not only greater physical health but also a far better quality of life.

Chapter 1 begins by relating the amazing story of Jay's recovery from cancer through a cleansing diet of raw fruit and vegetable juices, as well as his mission to share with others the remarkable healing power of juice therapy. It then discusses the many benefits of fresh juice, which, as you will learn, is a nutritional powerhouse that's bursting with vitamins, minerals, enzymes, and a wealth of other health-promoting substances. Finally, it offers a quick-start juice fast as a vital first step towards a living foods diet.

Chapter 2 focuses on an important aspect of the living foods diet—the power of green juices and green foods. It starts by exploring how the sun lends plants the awesome power of its energy, which is passed on to you when you drink fresh juices and eat wholesome foods in their raw state. A special section introduces you to high-nutrient "superfoods" such as chlorella and wheatgrass, and a ninety-day plan guides you in improving your diet gradually over three months.

Chapter 3 spotlights another essential topic: enzymes. First you will learn the important functions that enzymes carry out in the body. You will then discover the links between enzymes and raw foods, and—perhaps most important—you'll find guidelines for maximizing your enzyme power.

The diet we describe in this book—the one that we've been thriving on for decades —is a potent health-promoting, longevity-enhancing plan that has its roots in the power of living foods. In the following pages, you will learn how this diet can change your life forever.

1.

The Power of Juicing

I am often asked why I am so passionate about juicing. The answer is simple: It saved my life. Diagnosed with a bladder tumor at the age of twenty-five, I turned to Dr. Max Gerson—the leading authority on juice therapy—in hopes of improving my chances of survival. After only three months on Dr. Gerson's juice diet, my tumor was gone, and my life was changed forever. For more than sixty years, I have dedicated my life to teaching others about the power of juicing while continuing to follow the diet that led me to ultimate healing.

A strong grasp of juicing and its nutritional benefits is essential for understanding how *all* living foods—not just juiced fruits and vegetables—can transform your health. This chapter introduces you to juicing as one of the key elements of our vegan living foods program. Once you are familiar with the basics of juicing, you will be inspired to expand your consumption of living foods and adopt this empowering lifestyle.

"It is my view that the vegetarian manner of living, by its purely physical effect on the human temperament, would most beneficially influence the lot of mankind."

—ALBERT EINSTEIN, PHYSICIST

DISCOVERING JUICE THERAPY

In 1942, when I was a student and football player at the University of Southern California, I was called to serve in the Navy for three years during World War II. After returning to USC following the war, my athletic career was again put on hold due to a minor injury that benched me for a year. During that time, I became ill with a bladder problem that was later diagnosed as a tumor. By today's standards, cancer rates among Americans at that time were relatively low, and cancer treatments like chemotherapy and radiation were not yet fully developed. Thus, at the age of only twenty-five, I was told I had less than a year to live if I did not undergo treatment, and that the only plausible treatment option— surgery and cobalt therapy—would not guarantee a cure. I opted for an alternative.

Jay in naval uniform during World War II.

I had read about Dr. Max Gerson, a German holistic medical doctor who was treating terminally ill patients with cleansing diets of fresh raw juice. Although a popular health practice among Europeans, juicing was not well-known by most Americans in the 1940s. Nevertheless, I quickly went to visit Dr. Gerson's cancer treatment clinic in New York and began my three-month juice therapy program, consuming only raw juices. This was not an easy task for a former football player accustomed to eating fatty foods like steak, hamburgers, cakes, and pies. The first three weeks were almost unbearable. Yet, by the end of the fourth week, I felt my body, mind, and soul completely transform. I felt more alive and energetic. I lost weight, my skin cleared up, I was no longer constipated, and I could breathe clearly. Most importantly, I was no longer bleeding in the genital area, which had been the first symptom of the tumor. I began to have hope.

After three months on the program, Dr. Gerson gave me a thorough examination and discovered that the tumor had disappeared. He advised me to continue the Gerson diet for another three months. Afterwards, I would be able to gradually incorporate pure organic foods—mostly raw fruits and vegetables—into my dietary regimen. For the rest of my life, I would need to follow a vegetarian diet high in greens, and drink at least twenty-four ounces of carrot and apple juice daily. I have remained on this basic living-foods diet ever since, consuming mostly organic vegan foods, about 75 percent of which are raw (living). Now ninety years young, I am just as healthy and energetic as ever, and my tumor has never returned.

MY MISSION BEGINS

My health scare started me on a mission to teach others about the healing power of juice therapy. I gave up my studies at USC—unfortunately only a few credits short of my degree—as well as the possibility of a lucrative football career. And yet I have never regretted my decision. For more than sixty years, I have traveled across the United States sharing my story, extolling the virtues of juicing, and helping others discover juice therapy as a key to healing. Linda and I have been blessed with good health and vitality, without which money and success mean nothing. As I know firsthand, illness has a way of stopping everything in its tracks.

Over the years, we have seen juicing gain popularity in the United States. While it's encouraging that more people are now deciding to buy juicers, it's important that they know how to use them the right way. Without an understanding of juice therapy, owning a juicer is like having a car with an empty gas tank! Our goal is not just to motivate you to buy a juicer, but also to teach you how to maximize its ability to enhance your health.

Linda, Jay, and their sons.

For several decades, I have worked with some of the top experts in the field of juice therapy to keep our recipes and advice in step with the most current advances in nutrition. In addition to Dr. Gerson, I have been mentored by Dr. Gabriel Cousens, the world's leading authority on living foods and my own medical doctor. It was because of Dr. Cousens that I reduced the amount of apples in Dr. Gerson's

famous carrot and apple juice combination. Today, as Dr. Cousens has informed me, many varieties of vegetables and fruits—including apples—are hybridized (genetically altered) to enhance flavor, which often involves increasing their sugar content. Furthermore, thanks to the expertise of Dr. Norman Walker, the author of *Fresh Vegetable and Fruit Juices,* I now recommend limiting fruit juice intake to the morning for better blood sugar management, as well as using vegetable juices—specifically, a combination of Brussels sprouts and string beans—to improve blood sugar by stimulating natural insulin production.

Drs. Gerson, Cousens, and Walker didn't just lead me to natural healing; they inspired and furthered our mission to educate others about the power of juicing and living foods. Now that Drs. Gerson and Walker are gone, Linda and I feel an even greater responsibility to let people know about this transforming lifestyle.

WHY JUICE?

Fresh living juice is a veritable nutritional powerhouse, rich in vitamins, minerals, enzymes, and *phytochemicals,* or naturally occurring chemicals in plants. Only plants have the ability to directly absorb energy from the sun, which humans are able to obtain only by consuming plant foods like raw fruits and vegetables. As Dr. Norman Walker explains, "The rays of the sun send billions of atoms into plant life, activating the enzymes, and by this force, they change inorganic elements into organic or life-containing elements for food." Plants also "drink up" minerals, which are formed in the innermost layers of the earth's crust and present in soil, while vitamins and enzymes are manufactured in the cell walls of plant tissues. Each of these elements is literally bound within plants, locked into their living fibers.

New research shows that as much as 90 percent of fruits' and vegetables' nutritional value is contained not in their flesh or pulp, but in *pectin,* an insoluble fiber contained in the peels and skins of fruits and the cell walls of vegetables. This is what I means when I say, "It is the juice from the fiber

> ## TIP
> Fresh juice made at home should be consumed within an hour to retain the precious enzymes that are vital for energy and superior digestion. If you are unable to make your own juice due to time constraints, fresh juices can be found at many supermarkets, especially natural foods stores. Read nutrition labels carefully to make sure the juice is organic and not pasteurized, as pasteurization destroys enzymes and other nutrients. Juice bars are another way to obtain fresh raw juice. One of our favorite juice bars is Lanikai Juice, which is located in Kailua, Hawaii. If you ever find yourself in the neighborhood, stop by—they've got great juice combinations and fresh, tasty organic fruit.

that feeds you." Juicing is the key to unlocking and releasing the full spectrum of nutrients contained in both fruits and vegetables—especially the nutrients that are usually unavailable to humans due to our inability to digest, for example, watermelon rinds. This is precisely why a glass of fresh raw juice is the best source of instant nutrition. Providing you with the greatest amount of nutrients per calorie, fresh juice is Mother Nature in liquid form. When you cook fruits and vegetables, their inherent life force is extinguished.

Another benefit of juicing is that it enables nutrients to work quickly in your body. Nutrients are released immediately and rendered biologically active in about fifteen minutes. In addition, fruits and vegetables are self-digesting, which means the process does not require help from other enzymes and takes only about twenty minutes to complete. When the body is not forced to expend so much energy to digest food, you feel more alive, energetic, and ready to enjoy your life. By contrast, cooked fatty foods, like sinewy beef, can remain in your system for days, preventing the absorption of important nutrients, causing putrefaction (decomposition) in the intestinal tract, and often resulting in sluggishness. One of the greatest assets of juicing—and living foods diets in general—is its ability to accelerate the digestion and elimination process, in turn enhancing your overall health and quality of life.

Juicing is also the key to detoxifying and cleansing your body, which is crucial in an age of pervasive pollution and adulterated refined foods. Drinking fresh fruit and vegetable juices will give you a full-body makeover, rebuilding it inside and out and reviving your youth. As a bonus, freshly made juices are absolutely delicious. If you've never had "real" juice before, you're in for quite a treat. In our opinion, there's no better beverage on earth.

FOLLOWING A JUICE FAST

Now that you're familiar with all that juicing has to offer, we recommend that you cleanse your system with a juice fast— the first step towards a living foods diet. Linda and I have been doing regular juice fasts for many years, and find it to be a very powerful and cathartic experience that rejuvenates your whole body and mind. It takes discipline and faith, but the rewards are many. We usually fast once every six months for approximately seven days. Sometimes, we will fast for only three or four days, depending on how we feel. Even the season can play a role in how long we fast. The best way to determine the length of your fast is to listen carefully to your body, which you will become more attuned to with time.

If you are new to fasting, we recommend the Three-Day Quick-Start Juice Cleanse, a three-day starter program outlined in Table 1.1. Because blood sugar fluctuates during fasts, the program includes few fruit juices—mostly vegetable juices and organic herbal teas. You can use any of the juice combination recipes included in Table 1.2 for lunch, dinner, and your mid-afternoon snack, but for breakfast we recommend a specific combination, as indicated in Table 1.1. While you may use any type of apple that you wish, we recommend green apples—such as Granny Smith or Pippins—for people who are managing their blood sugar, as they are lower in sugar than other varieties. Also, when purchasing

TABLE 1.1. THE THREE-DAY QUICK-START JUICE CLEANSE	
Breakfast	24 ounces (711 milliliters) of fresh vegetable juice consisting of:
	4 stalks celery
	1 lime (with skin)
	1 cucumber, unwaxed
	1 cup parsley
	1 apple
Mid-morning	8 ounces (237 milliliters) of an organic herbal tea.
Lunch	24 ounces (711 milliliters) of any juice combination in Table 1.2.
Mid-afternoon	24 ounces (711 milliliters) of any juice combination in Table 1.2 *or* water.
Dinner	24 ounces (711 milliliters) of any juice combination in Table 1.2.
Evening	8 ounces (237 milliliters) of organic herbal tea, preferably chamomile.

tea, choose only organic herbal teas such as chamomile, ginger, and peppermint. Do not drink green tea and black tea, as they are very stimulating, and do not add sweeteners of any kind to either the juices or the teas.

Although this beginner program is great for most people, consult your health-care provider or medical doctor before you start. If you are diabetic, pre-diabetic, or have a problem with sugar tolerance, speak to your doctor about whether limits should be placed on high-sugar produce such as carrots and beets.

The recipes in Table 1.2 are great for beginners and yield approximately 24 ounces (711 milliliters) if you are using medium-sized produce. You may get a bit more than this amount if you use carrots, cucumbers, and other produce that is larger in size. Remember to wash your produce thoroughly before juicing so that any trace of fungus or bacteria is eliminated. (See page 153 for more juicing tips.)

TABLE 1.2. VEGETABLE JUICE COMBINATIONS FOR CLEANSES		
Juice Combination	**Ingredients**	
Carrot/Beet/Spinach/Celery	8 carrots	Handful spinach
	$^1/_4$ beet	2 stalks celery
Carrot/Cucumber/Cabbage	8 carrots	1 cup (100g) chunks green cabbage
	1 cucumber, unwaxed	
Carrot/Parsley/Spinach/Celery/Apple	8 carrots	2 stalks celery
	Handful parsley	1 apple
	Handful spinach	
Carrot/Chard/Spinach/Apple/Beet	8 carrots	1 apple
	2 leaves Swiss chard	$^1/_2$ beet
	1 cup spinach	
Collard Greens/Romaine lettuce/ Celery/Lime/Apple	3 collard greens	1 lime
	6 leaves romaine lettuce	1 apple
	4 stalks celery	

It's a good idea to fast at an opportune time, such as a three-day weekend, to ensure that your experience is as relaxing and enjoyable as possible. Below are some additional recommendations for a successful juice fast:

● Rid your kitchen of any tempting foods that may deter you from your commitment to the fast.

● In addition to the juices, be sure to drink plenty of water while fasting. You need about eight 10-ounce (295-milliliter) glasses of pure water daily. We recommend steam distilled water or water purified through reverse osmosis. Do not drink tap water, since it contains contaminants that can contribute to conditions like kidney stones. When dining out, be sure to ask your server for filtered water, even in beverages like iced tea. To make the water more alkaline, add a few drops of fresh organic lemon juice.

● Take a natural laxative every day to help move your bowels, since you will not be eating food. Be sure to meet your daily water requirement, as bowel cleansers tend to pull moisture from your body.

● Relax. A fast is meant to be a time of rest, meditation, and enjoying leisure activities like yoga and reading. If you must work, slow your pace. During the three days, you should engage in mild exercise, such as walking or stretching, and take time for yourself each evening. If possible, take a long hot sauna to speed detoxification. Linda likes to unwind after a long day by taking a warm bath with lavender oil, while I prefer a warm shower. Before bathing, use a dry body brush to massage your skin for five minutes. This stimulating action helps the skin breathe and enhances blood flow to your pores.

Following these guidelines will allow you to make the most of your fasting experience. Still, be aware that temporary side effects such as headaches, nausea, dizziness, bowel irregularity, skin breakouts, and increased irritability are possible. These side effects indicate that detoxification is taking place in the body and should subside within

> ## TIP
>
> When making a vegetable-juice tonic, we recommending juicing most of the firm vegetables first, and then alternating between leafy greens and any additional soft vegetables included in the recipe. Juice the remaining firm vegetables—such as leftover carrots—last. This method allows the tender greens and softer produce to flow through the juicer more quickly and efficiently. (For more juicing tips, see the inset on page 153 of Part Three.)

two or three days. If they do not disappear, speak to your physician.

After finishing the juice fast, congratulate yourself! You have accomplished something that few people are willing to try. Break your fast by eating light foods, such as salads without dressing and fruits, for the next few days. Do not eat heavy foods or regular-sized meals right away, since your body is still recovering from the effects of detoxification.

MAKING LIVING JUICES A PART OF YOUR LIFE

The three-day cleanse is not the end, but the beginning of your juicing regimen. After your fast, you should juice raw organic fruits and vegetables every day. We generally recommend that beginners start off with juice combinations that consist of about 50 to 75 percent carrots, with greens and apples making up the remainder. However, if you have diabetes, pre-diabetes, or any form of sugar intolerance, 25- to 50-percent carrots is a more appropriate range, as carrots are high in naturally occurring sugars. (If you have blood sugar issues, please consult your physician before starting to juice.) Gradually reduce the amount of carrots until they make up only 25 to 50 percent of your juices. If you cannot find organic carrots in your area or are sugar-sensitive, substitute cucumbers but cut the amount in half. For example, if a recipe calls for eight carrots, use four cucumbers instead.

Most of our juice recipes (see page 152) are for vegetable juices, as vegetables are more nutritionally dense than fruits. However, we include apples in many of the recipes because they sweeten the juices, helping you become accustomed to "green" tastes. In general, apples, lemons, and limes are the best fruits for improving the flavor of vegetable juice combinations, since their juices are compatible with vegetable oils. When you become more experienced at

> ## TIP
>
> One vegetable that you should be particularly careful when juicing is beets. As a rule, beets should make up no more than 30 percent of any juice. Beets are very cleansing, especially for the liver, and may produce side effects like gas and reddish urine or stools. If side effects persist, cut the amount of beets in your juice by half, and then gradually increase the amount to allow your body to adapt. Use beet greens only if you have been juicing vegetables (including beets) for at least thirty days. Beet greens are extremely detoxifying, so it's important to acclimate your body to them slowly.

juicing, it's best to gradually transition to drinking more heavily concentrated green juices, which have more healing properties. Some of the best greens and other vegetables to juice include:

- Bell peppers (red, orange, and yellow)
- Broccoli
- Brussels sprouts
- Cabbage (green or red)
- Celery
- Collard greens
- Cucumber, English (unwaxed) or regular
- Dandelion greens
- Kale
- Parsley
- Purslane
- Radish
- Romaine lettuce
- Spinach
- Swiss chard (green, red, and/or rainbow)
- Wheatgrass
- Yellow summer squash
- Zucchini

On the other hand, because fruits contain a significant amount of natural mineral water, we tend to eat most of them whole. Although some of our juice recipes include fruits that are rich in fiber, it's preferable to eat high-fiber fruits, as your body needs fiber in large amounts to function at an optimal level. There are plenty of other fruits that are perfect for juicing. In addition to apples, our favorite fruit-juice and fruit-smoothie ingredients include:

- Blackberries
- Blueberries
- Cantaloupes (skin included)
- Cherries
- Cranberries
- Grapefruits
- Kiwis
- Lemons
- Limes
- Pears
- Melons
- Raspberries

Although most of these fruits are low in sugar, you should speak to your doctor before consuming juiced fruits if you have any blood sugar issues. There is a whole section devoted to juice recipes in Part Three (see page 152). We encourage you to choose the ones that fit your food preferences and health needs, and experiment until you find the combinations that are right for you. Part Three also contains additional tips for effectively selecting, preparing, and juicing your produce.

CONCLUSION

It's important to treat your body well, and juicing is a vital first step towards optimal wellness. Stressful living and poor food choices diminish your health, but juicing—and juice fasting, in particular—can help you reduce stress, replenish your energy, and rejuvenate your body. Consuming fresh raw juices is a key element in a living foods diet, since they are packed with nutrients that vitalize your system. This inherent "life force" of organic fruits and vegetables—the quality that gives living foods diets their healing power—is discussed in the next chapter.

2.

Going Green

We underestimate the very powerful relationship between the environment and plant life because, quite frankly, most of us do not understand it. One of my favorite sayings is: "All life on planet Earth emanates from the green of the plant." Essentially, plants are the factories of life. Through photosynthesis, plants take in carbon dioxide, water, and sunlight to harness energy in the form of glucose and release oxygen. With their roots deeply planted in the ground, they draw inorganic elements and minerals from the soil, beautifully and naturally converting them into what could be called the life force. Green juices and foods derived from plant life supply us with abundant amounts of oxygen, chlorophyll, alkalinity, immunity, and water, keeping our cells alive and healthy. Simply put, green juices are utilized perfectly by the human body.

"All life on planet Earth emanates from the green of the plant."

—JAY KORDICH

THE ESSENCE OF LIFE

The magnificence of the sun sometimes goes beyond human understanding, but when you start to consume green foods, you will not only be overwhelmed by the immediate infusion of natural energy, you will also begin to revere this exceptional gift given to us every single day. Plants, and all life on Earth for that matter, require the sun's energy to survive. As previously stated, plants convert electromagnetic energy from the sun into chemical energy, or food. This chemical energy consists of protein, carbohydrates, essential fatty acids, vitamins, minerals, enzymes, antioxidants, and phytochemicals, as well as purified plant water, the most nutritious liquid on Earth.

Eating live plants and consuming their juices imbues the human body with the awesome power of the sun's energy. The late Dr. Maximilian Bircher-Benner of Europe's world-renowned Bircher-Benner clinic was one of the first to advance this truth. The doctor stated:

> Absorption and organization of sunlight, the essence of life, takes place almost exclusively within the plants. The organs of the plant are therefore a biological accumulation of light. They are the basis of what we call food, from whence humans derive their sustenance and energy. Nutritional energy may thus be termed organized sunlight energy. Hence, sunlight is the driving force of the cells of our body.

Given that our bodies require the sun's energy, and knowing that plants are the most available form of that energy, doesn't it follow that the most supreme nutrition for the

"Sunlight is the driving force of the cells of our body."
—MAXIMILIAN BIRCHER-BENNER, PHYSICIAN

human organism is living plants? Just like many other animals, humans have a persistent and perpetual need for the vital nutrients that Nature has provided in living plant cells. For the human body to function at optimal efficiency and achieve excellent health, it must be supplied with the basic chemicals of life. Our bodies cannot manufacture the nutrients we need. We must obtain them through diet.

PLANT POWER

It is so important to consume a variety of greens daily, either whole or as juice. You will be amazed by how great you feel when you incorporate dark leafy greens in your diet. They are the key to achieving vital energy and longevity. You could say that plants are our lifeblood. The food chain begins with plant life. In plants, Nature has brought together all the raw materials required to build and sustain life. Even plants that grow in the ocean, such as algae and seaweed, contain huge amounts of powerful super food nutrients. You can build a strong immune system, abundant with natural energy, by taking advantage of the power of plants.

"The first wealth is health."

—RALPH WALDO EMERSON, PHILOSOPHER AND AUTHOR

The Power of Nori

In countries such as Japan and China, greens from the sea are regularly consumed. One of the most popular is a seaweed called nori. Nori is rich in health-promoting minerals, vitamins, and phytochemicals. Available in most health food grocery stores and Asian markets, nori can be purchased cooked or uncooked. If it is green in color, it has not been cooked. If it is black in color, it has been toasted. If you are not used to eating seaweed, we suggest you try the toasted nori first, as its flavor is a bit easier to handle. When you get used to toasted nori, you can switch to the uncooked version, in which more of the vitamins, enzymes, and phytochemicals have been left intact.

THE IMPORTANCE OF RAW MATERIALS

In fresh fruits and vegetables, Nature has organized and made available all the raw materials necessary for human life. They are concentrated in the form of living cells. But as soon as vegetables or fruits are cooked, boiled, baked, processed, or pasteurized and bottled as commercial juice, they are stripped of a vital portion of their nutritive value. Cooking and refining renders them inferior forms of nutrition. It is the life force contained in living plants and their rich endowment of nutrients that sustains, nourishes, and regenerates all the tissues and organs of the human body. In order to be fully utilized as nourishment, these cells must be alive and vital, not cooked and dead. Live foods feed live bodies. Dead foods do not. I don't eat any cooked greens, and the only ones Linda consumes are steamed broccoli and green beans, which are harder to eat raw.

When we juice, of course, we do not cook the fruits and vegetables. If we did, the juice would lose its healing properties. For example, raw carrot and spinach juice (60 to 75 percent carrot and 25 to 40 percent spinach) has the power to ease many stomach ailments, including diarrhea, constipation, gas, cramps, ulcer-like symptoms, and stomachache. When spinach is cooked, though, its enzymes are destroyed and most of its vitamin and mineral content is compromised, resulting in a reduction of its healing abilities.

SUPERFOODS

Superfoods are plant-derived foods that offer a remarkably high amount of nutrients or contain particular health-giving properties over and above other fruits and vegetables. They are an important part of a healthy diet. The following are superfoods that we recommend you add to your diet. Because they can have a big impact, we encourage you to incorporate them into your routine slowly.

Chlorella

A type of green algae, chlorella has been popular as a supplement in Japan for years. It is valued for a complex of substances known as chlorella growth factor, or CGF. CGF promotes healing, enhances the immune system, detoxifies the body, and is an anti-aging tool. Chlorella also contains significant amounts of vitamins B_{12} and A, and is rich in chlorophyll, which has been shown to increase red blood cells. A greater number of red blood cells can promote better oxygenation of cells, which, in turn, may improve the body's removal of cellular waste.

Superfoods like chlorella and green barley are a concentrated source of important nutrients. Most are available in supplement form and can be added to juices and smoothies. The best way to benefit from wheatgrass, though, is to drink freshly prepared wheatgrass juice.

Green Barley

Green barley comes from barley grass and, like chlorella, is high in chlorophyll. It is rich in magnesium, potassium, beta-carotene, and vitamin C. While it is often used to relieve colds and flu, research has demonstrated its effectiveness in relieving skin disorders, protecting against radiation, repairing damaged cells, and treating chronic diseases of the pancreas.

Green barley may be juiced or purchased as a supplement in powder or tablet form. The powder can be dissolved in cool water, nut milk, or juice. It's best to start with a small amount of green barley in your diet, as it may cause diarrhea. Others may develop constipation when taking green barley essence because it is low in fiber. To avoid this reaction, simply eat vegetables at the same time that you use green barley.

Wheatgrass

Wheatgrass is actually young wheat leaves. When only a few inches in height, the tender blades can be juiced or turned into tablets, pellets, or powder. Wheat grass is high in chlorophyll; pro-vitamin A; vitamins B, C, and E; and the minerals calcium, potassium, magnesium, selenium, and zinc. It also contains some iron. Since the juice is easily assimilated without losing its nutrients, we think it best to drink your wheatgrass rather than consume it in a dehydrated form.

Spirulina

A tiny aquatic plant, spirulina boasts a high protein content plus an abundance of vitamins and minerals.

Spirulina is a form of blue-green microalgae, a tiny aquatic plant that can be seen only through a microscope. Spirulina's use as a supplement in the United States began in 1979, but its existence dates to the beginning of plant life on Earth. Its status as a superfood comes from the fact that it is 60 to 70 percent protein by weight, which is twice as high as the protein content of dried milk and almost a third higher than that of whole dried eggs or brewer's yeast.

Spirulina boasts high amounts of vitamin B_{12} and other B vitamins. It also contains biotin, pantothenic acid, folic acid, and inositol. In addition, the concentrated presence of gamma-linolenic acid (GLA) in spirulina has been shown to alleviate degenerative diseases like arthritis and heart disease. Although it is not promoted as a weight loss aid, people who take spirulina before meals seem to have greater control over their level of food intake.

Bee Pollen

Bee pollen is a mixture of pollen, bee digestive juices, and nectar. Bees deposit bee pollen into the waxy cells of the hive, where it becomes their primary protein source. Bee pollen, like spirulina, is a rich source of protein—about 23 percent by weight. It is low in fat and sodium, and is a good source of beta-carotene, B vitamins (except B_{12}), calcium, magnesium, and zinc. It also has a moderate amount of vitamin C.

Bee pollen is known to help problems of the prostate. While this supplement can be bought in tablet and pellet

forms, the best type is fresh pollen granules from a local bee-keeper. Buying pollen directly from a beekeeper helps ensure that it has been collected by bees in an organic, toxin-free locale. When this is not possible, pollen pellets are best. Be sure to store fresh pollen in the refrigerator.

TIME FOR A CHANGE

By changing your diet slowly—over a period of ninety days—you will enable your body to more easily adjust to its new "fuel," and dietary change is likely to be more permanent.

Because most of us follow a diet that includes far more animal products than plants, it's no wonder we are exhausted by the time we are forty, sick by the time we turn fifty, and physically degenerated by the time we reach sixty. Most of us have only small amounts of vital energy left by the time we get to seventy or, luckily, eighty. If we stay close to Nature by consuming the foods we were meant to eat, such as fruits, nuts, grains, seeds, legumes, vegetables, and herbs, we will then have the energy and vitality to sustain us well into our nineties and beyond. We need to simplify our lives and change our eating habits. Don't you think it is time for a change?

GOING GREEN IN NINETY DAYS

Slow and steady wins the race. When you take it slow, the changes you make will feel more natural and be more permanent. Before you follow the diet outlined in this book, it would be wise to give yourself a great start by changing your everyday food choices over a ninety-day period.

Days One to Thirty

Begin your ninety-day period by eliminating fast food from your daily routine. In addition, remove the following from your diet:

❏ 25 percent of your daily alcohol, coffee, meat, and dairy consumption

❏ 50 percent of your daily soda consumption

❏ Artificial ingredients

❏ Fried food

❏ Refined sugar and flour

❏ Tap water

❏ White rice

When it comes to dairy products, keep yogurt in your diet, but make sure it contains live cultures such as bifidus and acidophilus.

Days Thirty to Sixty

After the first thirty days of your transition, you can continue to remove unhealthy items from your diet, including the following:

❏ Breads that contain yeast and dough conditioners, or hydrogenated oils

❏ An additional 25 percent of your starting daily alcohol, coffee, meat, and dairy consumption

❏ The rest of your daily soda consumption

In addition, take part in outdoor activities for at least ten hours a week.

Days Sixty to Ninety

During the last thirty days of your warm-up to going green, a final reduction of unhealthy foods is recommended. You should now cut out the following:

❏ An additional 25 percent of your starting daily alcohol, coffee, and meat consumption

❏ The rest of your daily dairy consumption

Although giving up some of these foods may seem drastic, substitutions can be made for many of your favorite foods and cooking methods. For example, use date or coconut sugar, stevia, honey, or rice syrup instead of refined

"Each patient carries his own doctor inside him."
—NORMAN COUSINS, AUTHOR

sugar. Bake or steam foods instead of frying them. Drink steam-distilled water or water purified through reverse osmosis rather than tap water. Replace coffee with beverages such as Teeccino, green tea, or Pero. Opt for freshly juiced fruits and vegetables rather than soda. Replace dairy with similar products made from soy or nuts. Instead of meat, choose tofu, tempeh, beans, or other vegetarian meat substitutes.

LEARNING TO LOVE GREENS

So, you say you don't like greens? Perhaps you have bad memories of your parents making you eat your vegetables at dinnertime. Linda sure has a few. From the time she was seven years old, her father would say, "If you don't eat your carrots and string beans, you'll sit at this dinner table until midnight, and then some!" In fact, Linda could not tolerate cooked carrots until she turned forty! When she married me, a devout carrot lover, she thought God was playing a joke on her. (At least I don't cook the carrots!) Over time, she adjusted her negative feelings about carrots and other vegetables, and so should you.

Years ago, I would tell people, "You will start to crave green salads if you can consume them on a daily basis for five to seven days." The transformation, however, may take up to ten days, depending on how your body reacts to the change. Once you start to consume greens on a daily basis, your body will begin to detoxify itself, which can be alarming for some. Toxins build up over many years, and a purifying diet may cause some initial discomfort as these substances leave your system. Within the first five days of eating greens regularly, you may notice an increase in bowel movements, acne, and slight headaches. These are signs of detoxification. If you experience any of these negative reactions, be patient; they will pass within a week. If they do not, we suggest you lighten up on the greens until your body adjusts to your new diet.

When it comes to eating your daily vegetables, if you or your children are like Linda used to be, juicing can help. Combine a few vegetables with an apple, put them through

If your kids balk at the idea of eating vegetables, try juicing them! Add a few carrots or an apple for sweetness, and your whole family will be sure to love the results.

your juicer, and you've got a beverage everyone is sure to love. Carrots and greens also make a deliciously sweet choice. Your children will be surprised by how tasty these juices can be. If you find the color of vegetable juice unappealing, simply pour your drink into an opaque glass.

By incorporating greens into your everyday life, you will wake up each morning with a natural energy that will last throughout the day. This routine will calm your nerves and encourage a gentler approach to life.

CONCLUSION

Once you "go green," you will begin to feel a tremendous freedom from the unhealthy foods you once included in your diet. Before long, you will lose not only your addiction to these foods but also the weight they caused you to gain over the years! Most people lose around five to ten pounds during the first couple of months of switching to a diet rich in living foods. Perhaps due to the sense of empowerment that follows seeing this physical change, at this point, most people have completely broken their old dietary habits. Regardless, if you ever slip up and indulge in unhealthy food choices again, the knowledge that this lifestyle can have a positive effect on your body will help you return to your healthy ways. By eating a diet high in raw fruits and vegetables, both whole and juiced, and taking advantage of the superfoods mentioned in this chapter, you will open a door to a hopeful future and recognize that health is your greatest wealth. Don't you think this lifestyle is worth a try? Vital health awaits you.

3.

Enzymes— The Key to Vitality

T he single most important difference between living and cooked foods is the presence of *enzymes*, substances that act as catalysts for practically every biochemical reaction that occurs in the body. Breathing, blinking, hearing, seeing, and smelling are all governed by enzyme activity. Enzymes are also required for vital functions such as digestion, nutrient absorption, immunity, and organ function. Simply put, enzymes are absolutely necessary for life.

Although the body has its own enzyme supply, it's essential to take in enzymes through dietary sources as well. Food enzymes—which are naturally present in living foods like fruits, vegetables, and grains—enhance digestion, allowing the body to hold on to its internal enzymes and conserve energy. The importance of enzymes cannot be overstated, yet most people are unaware of their nutritional value and vast health benefits. This chapter provides a general overview of enzymes and the key role they play in a living foods diet. It also offers advice on how to maximize the enzyme power contained in the raw foods you eat, so that you can improve your energy level, quality of life, longevity, and overall health.

The key difference between living foods and cooked foods is that only living foods provide your body with enzymes—natural substances that allow the body to perform thousands of vital functions, including digestion.

THE BIOLOGICAL ROLE OF ENZYMES

From the moment of conception, there is enzyme activity in

human beings. Enzymes are biological catalysts responsible for initiating, directing, or accelerating every chemical process that occurs in the body. They are your body's "workers," and in order for your system to operate at top efficiency, you need an abundant supply. To date, science has identified approximately 3,200 enzymes—and that is likely just the tip of the iceberg. One enzyme helps build phosphorus in bones. Another causes muscles to contract. Yet another enzyme is responsible for the clotting mechanism in blood. Fear, hunger, and sexual arousal are all controlled by powerful enzymes in the brain. The importance of enzymes is undeniable; they embody the mysterious life force upon which every living thing thrives.

Perhaps most important of all is the role enzymes play in food digestion and the absorption of nutrients. Before nutrients can be absorbed and utilized, your food must be broken down into simpler building blocks and reformulated based on your body's needs. These building blocks are used to restore old worn-out cells in every part of the body. Enzymes are the driving force behind this vital process, giving your body the nutrients it needs to remain alive.

YOUR BODY'S ENZYME "BANK ACCOUNT"

All human beings are born with a fixed amount of enzymes—a kind of personal enzyme "bank account." Typically, the younger you are, the greater your enzyme reserves. *Metabolic enzymes* exist in your organs, blood, and bones, as well as each of your cells. These enzymes are essential for cell growth and tissue maintenance, and help each part of your body carry out its respective functions. *Digestive enzymes,* which are actually a specific type of metabolic enzyme, are responsible solely for facilitating digestion, thereby allowing nutrients to be absorbed and released into the bloodstream. The pancreas produces most of your body's digestive enzymes.

A diet high in processed foods forces your body to rely on its enzyme "bank account" and, over time, depletes your enzyme stores. But a diet high in living foods makes regular deposits in your account, boosting your body's performance and function.

Since digestion requires the body to expend a great deal of energy, your natural enzyme supply is not sufficient—you must add to your "bank account" by eating a diet rich in *food enzymes,* which are found only in raw (living) foods like fruits, vegetables, and grains. Dairy foods do not contain natural enzymes, but rather bioengineered versions that are added to certain products, like cheese, to improve texture or flavor. Processed foods and pasteurized juices are also devoid of enzymes. Furthermore, baking and cooking foods—even fruits, vegetables, and grains—at temperatures higher than 115°F (46°C) destroys nearly all of their enzymes, as well as their fiber content (see the inset on page 38). Placing foods in boiling water also strips them of their enzymes.

Eating a diet of mostly enzyme-less foods forces your body to rely solely on its internal reserves to carry out vital functions. The pancreas must work overtime, cranking out extra enzymes needed to process denatured and devitalized foods and move them through the digestive tract. As a result, the pancreas is deterred from its other functions, including insulin secretion and the production of enzymes that inhibit the development of trophoblastic (precancerous) cells. Generally, this effect is of little consequence in young people, whose bodies have a wealth of natural enzymes. This is also why young people can usually tolerate diets high in unhealthy cooked foods like white bread and pasta, baked goods, animal products, high-sugar foods such as

Cooking Destroys Fiber-Rich Foods

In addition to enzymes, fruits and vegetables contribute much-needed fiber to your body. When food is eaten in a living, unprocessed state, any fiber it contains acts like a broom in your intestines and colon, sweeping away harmful bacteria and keeping the digestive tract clean. However, high-heat cooking devitalizes the fiber in food so that its action is more mop-like, which often leaves a coating of slime on your intestinal walls. Over time, this slime accumulates and putrefies, ultimately causing *intestinal toxemia*, a disorder that is discussed below. As a result, the colon becomes sluggish, which leads to constipation, colitis, diverticulitis, and other digestive disturbances.

If you have colon trouble, we suggest experimenting with a thirty-day colon cleanse. Colon cleanses improve your body's food absorption mechanism. Speak to your doctor or health practitioner before doing any kind of deep cleanse.

soda, and processed foods. Over the years, however, as enzyme reserves decrease, these same foods can cause problems such as constipation, bleeding ulcers, bloating, and digestive disorders like colitis and leaky gut syndrome. These are all symptoms of *intestinal toxemia*—also called *increased intestinal permeability*—an internal infection caused by the incomplete digestion of fats and foods in the intestinal tract.

On the other hand, if you consume mostly living foods and juices—which are loaded with natural plant food enzymes—you make regular deposits into your enzyme "bank account." This boosts not only your nutrition, but also your body's overall performance and function.

ENZYMES AND NUTRITION

When you eat living foods, your cells are infused with enzymes, increasing your body's vitality, energy, and stamina. These living foods are bursting with enzymes required for digestion, which work quickly and efficiently to break down the millions of cells in fruits, vegetables, herbs, grains, and other living foods that you eat. Fresh pineapple, for example, contains the powerful enzyme *bromelain;* bananas are rich in *amylase;* and the enzyme *papain* is found in papaya. Whenever you eat raw fruits and vegetables, their naturally occurring enzymes do most of the digestive work, breaking foods down into their more basic components in the stomach and small intestine. This means that enzymes in your body's internal reserves can be used for other activities, such as rebuilding damaged tissues and cells, bolstering your immune system, and other important functions. As a result, your body conserves energy. If enzymes are not present in your food, your system cannot efficiently digest or extract essential nutrients. This leaves your body nutrient-deprived and starved. That's one of the reasons we recommend that your diet ultimately be comprised of about 75 percent living foods. This percentage of living foods guarantees the abundance of enzymes that will allow you to digest your cooked foods more efficiently.

Dr. Edward Howell, who dedicated more than forty years of his life to enzymology, was one of the first researchers to prove the necessity of living food enzymes in human nutrition. Dr. Norman Walker, my mentor since 1948, summarized the importance of enzymes in the following way:

> Life as LIFE cannot be explained, so we describe enzymes as a Cosmic Energy Principle or vibration which promotes a chemical action or change in atoms and molecules, causing a reaction, without changing, destroying, or using up the enzymes themselves in the process. . . . By supplying our body daily with the elements of which it is composed, we can have complete health. . . .

"Living" is synonymous with "enzyme-rich." That's why we recommend that about 75 percent of your diet be comprised of living foods.

In other words, when you follow a living foods diet, you get the enzymes you need for optimal health, which helps you avoid premature aging and disease. "Living" is synonymous with "enzyme-rich."

YOUR ENZYME-RICH DIET

Asking yourself, "How much of my meal is alive?" is another way of asking, "How much of my meal is rich in enzymes?" Paying attention to the amount of raw food in your diet will forever change the way you look at and feel about food. When at least 75 percent of the food you eat comes from fruits, vegetables, nuts, seeds, herbs, and grains, in addition to feeling relaxed and balanced, you will enjoy tremendously improved digestion.

If less than 75 percent of your diet is living, we recommend that you consume up to one quart (one liter) of vegetable juices per day, or that you supplement your diet with digestive enzymes. You can find quality enzyme supplements on our website, which is listed in the Resources section (see page 209). Another option is to add chopped raw onions, chives, or fresh (uncooked) crushed garlic to your cooked meals. (See page 140 for acceptable cooked meal recipes.) Adding these natural enzyme-rich ingredients makes cooked food more "alive" and aids digestion. Plus, compounds present in raw onions and garlic help destroy foreign bacteria and parasites, and also keep the colon clean. (See the inset on page 43 for more tips on enhancing digestion.)

By juicing fruits and vegetables, you can take in even more enzymes. Freshly made juices are essentially predigested food, with nearly all of the nutrients and enzymes intact. When you juice a carrot, for example, you give your body an automatic enzyme boost—an extra shot of living, usable enzymes ready to go to work. The enzymatic benefits of juicing are also why we recommend drinking our Digestive Juice Aids (see page 164) with your meals. Rich in enzymes, these juices are specially designed to help you digest any meal that is less than 75-percent living.

MAXIMIZING YOUR ENZYME POWER

Enzymes need a proper environment in order to function at their very best. On the next page, you'll find ten guidelines for multiplying your body's enzyme reserves while maximizing their healthful life-sustaining benefits.

> **TIP**
>
> Enzyme supplements can be used to relieve digestive ailments, such as colitis and diarrhea, which may be induced by eating an abundance of greens. If you experience these problems, ask your health practitioner about enzyme therapy. Thousands of people have been helped tremendously by integrating this practice into their everyday life. Taking probiotics, healthy bacteria that boost intestinal health, can also help digestive issues.

1. Begin each day with fresh seasonal fruit or your favorite fresh fruit juice combination. Our favorite juice is a pineapple-grapefruit combination (see our Tropical Medley on page 173), which packs a punch of enzyme power. Pineapples and grapefruit are available year-round in most regions of the United States. Remember to always peel the grapefruit before juicing, and try to leave as much of its white pulp intact as possible. Starting your day this way gives your digestive system a powerful enzyme boost.

2. For lunch, have a "living" meal paired with fresh vegetable juice. We recommend a vegetable-based salad with a glass of Meal Sipper Digestive (see page 167). If your salad contains any cooked foods, the juice will give your body all the extra enzymes it needs to ensure smooth and easy digestion.

3. With the exception of apples and cantaloupes, do not mix fruits and vegetables in juices or meals. Because the enzymes found in fruits and vegetables are, for the most part, chemically incompatible, if you combine these foods in juices or meals, you may experience indigestion and, more important, difficulty in absorbing nutrients.

4. Limit the amount of liquid you drink with meals. Consuming too much liquid during meals can actually "drown" enzymes, diluting their power in the stomach and inhibiting their catalytic actions. It is acceptable to drink our Digestive Juice Aids (see page 164), but do not drink coffee, soda, fruit juice, or even water at mealtimes.

5. Restrict your intake of cooked foods. By "cooked foods," we mean any food subjected to temperatures higher than 115° F (46° C). If you must cook, the best methods are steaming and baking. Stay away from boiled foods, broiled foods, and fried foods. Also, never eat any cooked foods late at night. Your body needs rest from digestion at night to conduct other activities, like internal cleansing and repairs. If you tie up your enzymes for late-night digestion, your body will not be able to recuperate. You're better off having a cup of warm tea or a calming glass of enzyme-rich apple/celery juice before you retire. When in season, crisp organic apples or ripe pears are great to eat in the evening if you become hungry after dinner. Staying away from cooked food at night will ensure that you wake up with a clear head and clear eyes.

> One great way to maximize your enzyme power is to drink only natural beverages that are free of caffeine, carbonation, and other harmful substances. Freshly made juices are best, but you can also enjoy nut milk, rice milk, herbal tea, and other healthy alternatives.

6. Drink only natural beverages, preferably freshly made juices. Avoid coffee, alcohol, soda, and carbonated beverages of any kind, as well as sweetened beverages. Alcohol and caffeine destroy digestive juices and prevent enzyme production. However, you can still drink organic herbal teas. Replace coffee with substitutes like Teeccino, Cafix, and Pero, which are 100-percent caffeine-free and can be sweetened with honey or other natural sweeteners. (See the discussion of sweeteners below.) Freshly made soy milk, rice milk, and nut milk are also acceptable beverage choices. (See our nut milk recipes on page 183 of Part Three.) For the first six months of your living foods diet, be sure to drink plenty of pure water. We recommend steam-distilled water or water purified through reverse osmosis. Just make sure to have the water from your filtering system tested. It is not expensive and is well worth the effort, as it can alert you to any chemicals that remain in your water after filtering. *Never* drink tap water, even when dining at a restaurant. Ask your server for filtered water.

7. Avoid refined sugars. Not only does do refined sugars hinder enzyme activity, but they also interfere with healthy metabolism and contribute to heart disease. If you want to sweeten a beverage, use organic raw honey, which is full of powerful enzymes; coconut or date sugar, which are available in both granular and liquid form; and stevia, which is also available as a powder or liquid. Linda and I prefer coconut sugar. Just make sure that your sweetener is organic.

8. **Eat your biggest meal in the middle of the day.** Most people are more physically active during the day than at night, so it's important to eat your biggest meal when your digestive system is operating at top efficiency. As the old adage goes, "When the sun is highest in the sky, our digestive powers are at their greatest." If you sleep soon after a meal, your body—particularly your liver—suffers, so try to remain active for at least an hour after you eat.

9. **Chew your food extremely well.** A doctor friend used to tell us, "Chew your foods extremely well, at least thirty-two times per mouthful." This was known as Fletcherizing, named after the doctor, Horace Fletcher, who first advocated this method of chewing at the turn of the twentieth century.

Jay's Quick Tips for Better Digestion

The digestion of cooked food requires more energy and enzymes than the digestion of living food. For this reason, it's important to aid the digestive process however you can when eating cooked meals. As mentioned on page 40, supplementing with enzymes or adding enzyme-rich ingredients to your food is a great option. Below are a few additional ways to reduce your body's digestive work.

☐ Drink a glass of a freshly made Digestive Juice Aid with every cooked or semi-cooked meal. Sip it while slowly chewing your food and swish it around in your mouth. (See page 164 of Part Three for recipes.)

☐ If you find it difficult to digest nuts and grains, soak them overnight before cooking them. If you forget to do this, soak them for at least one hour prior to preparing the meal. Be sure to rinse nuts and grains after soaking. This action neutralizes their enzyme inhibitors, making the food much more digestible.

☐ Make meal preparation a relaxing experience. Light a candle and use the time to meditate, reflect, and, if you are religious, pray. This will reduce the tension that sometimes accompanies meal preparation.

Slow, thorough chewing releases more enzymes and helps predigest food, thereby preventing fatty wastes from being unnecessarily deposited in your cells. Thorough chewing also allows for better nutrient absorption and makes the digestive process easier for your body. When drinking Digestive Juice Aids with a cooked meal, always "chew" the first few mouthfuls by swishing it around in your mouth until it tastes sweet. This process helps the salivary glands and taste buds secrete *ptyalin,* an amylase, which is similar to an enzyme. Ptyalin initiates the breakdown of carbohydrates into simple sugars and starches, ensuring that you extract the full nutritional value of your meal. Drinking Digestive Juice Aids with your meals reduces the necessary amount of chewing by at least 70 percent.

10. Drink juice immediately after preparation. Due to a process called *oxidation,* enzymes in juice begin to evaporate when juice is left sitting for five minutes or more. Therefore, it's important to drink your juice as soon as possible after juicing. If you want to drink your juice away from home, rinse a stainless steel-lined thermos with water (tap water is okay for this), and keep it in the freezer overnight. When you take it out the next morning, you will notice that the inside of the thermos is frosted. This frosted lining preserves the enzyme content of freshly made juice for four to six hours, or until the lining thaws.

For best results, drink your homemade juice immediately after preparation. This will help keep enzymes and nutrients intact.

Sticking to a diet of mostly living foods is essential for giving your body the enzymes it needs. Still, your eating habits—including how and when you eat—have a huge impact on your enzyme count, as well as how efficiently the enzymes work in your body. Following the ten easy rules above will allow you to make the most of the enzymes in your food, putting you on the fast track to better health.

CONCLUSION

While there continues to be more and more groundbreaking research on the wonders of food enzymes, there is still so much to learn—and this chapter has just scratched the surface. In the future, scientists may be able to prove that enzymes enhance vitamin and mineral absorption, and that an enzyme-rich diet is the key to a disease-free life. The integral role that enzymes play in both nutrition and overall health is a basic biological fact that everyone should know and understand.

As we mentioned earlier, it's important to ask yourself, "How much of my meal is alive?" before eating. The more attuned you are to your eating habits, the more likely you are to make sure that you eat living foods rich in enzymes. In addition, being conscious of your food choices will enable you to adjust more quickly to our living foods program, which we explore in Part Two.

PART TWO

Following the Living Foods Lifestyle

I n Part One, you learned about the many benefits offered by a living foods diet. Part Two brings you a step closer to greater health by explaining how you can go about adopting this wonderful lifestyle.

Your transition to better eating begins in Chapter 4, which examines issues that are of importance to anyone who wants to eat more living foods. Within these pages, you will learn how to determine the percentage of your dishes that should be comprised of living foods, which cooked foods can be included in your daily menus, how you can successfully combine raw veggies and fruits with cooked ingredients, and much, much more. If you have questions about the best way to start your living foods adventure, you're sure to find the answers here.

Because the kitchen plays a central role in any food plan, Chapter 5 focuses on this very important part of your home. With the goal of creating a space that supports your new diet, the chapter guides you in assessing your present kitchen appliances and tools; eliminating unnecessary, potentially harmful kitchen equipment; and adding vital equipment. Through a "Living Foods Shopping List," the chapter also guides you to the best ingredients, from fresh produce to pantry items, for your living menus. Finally, to help ensure your success, it offers practical strategies for buying, washing, and storing your fruits and veggies on market day. These strategies will take the stress out of meal preparation and help you create wholesome living meals in no time flat, even when life gets hectic.

Although the benefits of live foods are enormous, there's no doubt that the process of replacing old dietary habits with new ones can be a little intimidating. The following chapters will ease your transition by giving you the general guidelines and specific tactics you need to succeed.

4.

Embracing the Living Foods Diet

Back in the 1960s, when vegetarianism was uncommon, I was startled to hear my mother proudly announcing to the family, "We are all going to be vegetarians!" Shortly thereafter, my mother also discovered the power of juicing fresh vegetables. I still recall coming home from junior high school, racing up the front steps, and hearing the juicer whirring. At that age, I wasn't exactly fond of drinking vegetable juices, but my mother was smart enough to encourage these eating habits, believing (correctly) that I would come to love them. Years later, as fate would have it, juicing brought my mother in contact with Jay Kordich, whom she met by attending one of his seminars at a local health food store. Not long after that, I met Jay as well, and my life changed forever. Jay and I began our relationship by talking about working together and soon realized that we were also meant to *be* together. We decided to marry and travel the United States, teaching as many people as possible about the wonderful benefits of juice therapy and the vegetarian lifestyle. Within days, our lifelong mission to promote juicing and natural foods had begun.

With my strong background in vegetarianism and juicing and Jay's role as the "father of juicing," it was only natural for living foods to become the center of our universe. While Jay first revealed the benefits of juicing to the world, together we would spread the word about the power of the living foods diet!

"Nature itself is the best physician."

—HIPPOCRATES, ANCIENT GREEK PHYSICIAN

WHAT ARE LIVING FOODS?

Living foods are plant foods such as nuts, seeds, herbs, fruits, and vegetables (including greens) in their raw form. The sun bakes plant foods to perfection, so it is best to consume most of them just as they are. In this way, all their life-giving vitamins, minerals, and enzymes are preserved, making their healthful properties more available and easily digested. When plant foods are cooked above 115°F (46° C), however, almost all of their enzymes are destroyed and their nutrients are degraded, critically diminishing the vitality of these substances.

While most plant foods are perfect in their natural state, certain vegetables, such as broccoli, cauliflower, and green beans, can benefit from a bit of steaming. This makes them easier to chew and helps remove any hidden fungus that could be present. One or two minutes of cooking in a steamer are all it takes to properly cook these foods. The vegetables become crisp-tender and retain most of their health-giving properties. When cooking broccoli, make sure to remove the broccoli from the cooker when it is still bright green in color. Once the color has faded, most of the nutrients have vanished.

The benefits of incorporating a large percentage of living foods in your daily regimen are nearly endless. Your stamina may increase and your bowel habits may change in a very positive, "regular" way. What's more, your skin may start to improve, and natural weight loss will very likely occur. But the most rewarding development is the natural sense of calmness and serenity you will attain. This relaxed attitude will lighten your spirit, and your addictions to unhealthy foods such as sugar, caffeine, and various processed products will begin to disappear!

You will start to notice big changes within two to three weeks of following this program, and within a few months, you will have overcome all your poor eating habits. Just remember, if you fall back into the bad routine of eating sugar, caffeine, and processed foods (which may happen), don't beat yourself up about it. As quickly as possible, get back to your living foods program, which will once again

The benefits of a living foods diet can include better overall health, improved digestion, natural weight loss, increased stamina, more radiant skin, and a greater sense of calmness.

help you overcome these addictions. Don't waste time worrying over a mistake or a lapse in judgment.

THE PERCENTAGE PRINCIPLE

After decades of study, Jay and I have learned that eating a primarily raw vegan diet is crucially important to vital health, stamina, and youthful energy. While we are convinced that eating a diet rich in raw, living foods is optimal, we are not advocating eating only raw foods. For most people, a completely raw diet just isn't a sustainable way of life. Blending your present lifestyle with your new dietary choices is the key to success. A diet of 100 percent living foods may not work for you, but incorporating a larger percentage of living foods into your diet is an attainable goal.

We suggest using this percentage principle to transition to a living foods diet that you can follow for life. Depending on the state of your health and your eating habits, you will begin by incorporating a certain amount of raw foods into your meals, gradually increasing this amount until you are at a level that is both health-promoting and sustainable. The test on page 52 will help you determine how to make a comfortable transition to a living foods lifestyle.

By the way, when Jay and I refer to suitable cooked foods, we don't mean lunch meat or cookies! Acceptable cooked foods include lightly steamed vegetables, cooked soups, tofu, legumes, and cooked grains such as brown rice, bulgur, millet, pearl barley, quinoa, oats, and couscous. (For cooked foods recipes, turn to page 140.) We suggest mixing the grains right into a salad. You'll be tickled pink by how delicious and satisfying a salad can be with the simple addition of a cooked grain, or even nuts, seeds, or cooked beans. We do not recommend white rice, which has been stripped of its nutritive value.

Keeping these grains on hand supports your ability to create an entire meal within minutes. It's wise to rinse thoroughly and soak these grains in steam-distilled or purified water the night before, or at least two hours before cooking. Steel-cut oats, however, need to be soaked for only about an hour. Soaking is extremely important because it eliminates

Ultimately, living foods should make up most of your diet. But a healthy food plan can also include lightly steamed vegetables, tofu, cooked soups, and cooked legumes and whole grains.

TAKE THE TEST

How Alive Are You?

In Part Three, you'll find a wealth of recipes, each of which is marked with the percentage of living foods in that dish—100 percent, 80 percent, etc. When you decide to switch to a living foods diet, you should choose the percentage of living foods based on your current diet and lifestyle. The healthier your diet and lifestyle are now, the more likely it is that your body will be able to tolerate dishes that are high in raw foods right from the start. If, on the other hand, you are now eating few raw foods and also have unhealthy lifestyle habits such as smoking and drinking alcohol, your body will need a longer time to adjust to raw fruits and veggies.

To determine the best way to start your new diet, answer all of the questions below by circling the answer that best reflects your lifestyle, and total your score based on the directions provided on page 54. Once you have your total, you will learn which percentage of living foods is right for your transition diet. For the purpose of this test, a serving is considered about $1/2$ cup.

1. How many servings of green foods— green veggies, green-based soups, green supplements, and super-green protein bars—do you now consume each day?

   A. 3 servings.

   B. Less than 3 servings.

   C. None.

2. How much vegetable juice do you drink each day?

   A. More than 32 ounces (about 1 L).

   B. Less than 32 ounces (about 1 L).

   C. None.

3. How many servings of fresh fruit do you eat each day?

   A. 5 servings or more.

   B. 3 servings or less.

   C. None.

4. How much raw (living foods) salad do you eat each day?

   A. More than 1 serving.

   B. Less than 1 serving.

   C. None.

5. How much time do you spend exercising each day?

   A. More than 30 minutes.

   B. Less than 30 minutes.

   C. None.

6. How much water do you consume each day?

   A. More than 96 ounces (about 3 L).

   B. Less than 96 ounces (about 3 L).

   C. Less than 50 ounces (about 1.5 L).

7. About how much of each day are you stressed?

   A. Pretty relaxed most of the time.

   B. Stressed about half of the time.

   C. Stressed more than half of the time.

8. How much meat do you consume each day?

   A. None.

   B. Less than 10 ounces (280 g).

   C. More than 10 ounces (280 g).

9. What quantity of dairy products do you consume daily?

   A. None.

   B. Less than 10 ounces (280 g).

   C. More than 10 ounces (280 g).

10. How much do you smoke each day?

    A. Not at all.

    B. Less than 1 pack.

    C. More than 2 packs.

11. How much alcohol—including wine and beer—do you drink each day?

    A. None.

    B. Less than 2 drinks.

    C. More than 2 drinks.

12. How many antacids do you take each day?

    A. None.

    B. Less than 2.

    C. More than 2.

13. How often do you have trouble digesting salads?

    A. Hardly ever.

    B. Occasionally.

    C. Most of the time.

enzyme inhibitors from the food, allowing for much better absorption and digestion. Pre-soaking should also be used in the preparation of legumes.

Try purchasing an automatic rice maker in which you can make various types of grains, including brown rice. It's easy to prepare your grains the night before with this appliance. (Purchase only high-quality appliances, though. Cheaper models will contain an aluminum body. Jay and I are very wary of using any product containing aluminum or a nonstick coating, which may leach into the food.)

VEGETARIAN CHOICES

Research has proven that the longest-living cultures, such as the Okinawans and the Hunzas, eat a predominately vegetarian diet. Following a vegetarian lifestyle seems to help individuals avoid many of the diet-related diseases that occur with age. Veganism has been a happy, healthy choice for us, but this doesn't mean that we insist that you become a vegan or even a vegetarian. Your goal may simply be to incorporate more living plant foods into your daily meals while cutting down on animal products.

There are several kinds of vegetarian regimens. If you already are a vegetarian, you may be interested in trying a different form of vegetarianism. The following is a list of various vegetarian eating styles and the types of food eaten within those practices:

❑ **Fruitarian.** Consumes only fruit, nuts, seeds, and berries. Fruitarians eat only plant foods that can be harvested from the plant without killing it. Some fruitarians also eat cooked grains.

A vegan diet has proved to be a healthy, happy choice for us. But if this dietary option is not for you, simply try to include more living plant foods in your daily meals.

Eating According to the Seasons

Seasons have a way of naturally telling us what to eat. For example, in October, when pears, pomegranates, and squashes are in season, we automatically know that we should be eating more of them. Likewise, during the summer months, it is time to consume perfectly ripe foods like peaches, cherries, berries, green beans, and tomatoes. Eating according to the seasons is very important to us. During the fall and winter, we tend to eat meals comprised of 75 percent living foods and 25 percent cooked foods. During the spring and summer, we usually follow a diet made up of 80 percent living foods and 20 percent cooked foods.

Veganism for You and the Planet

Raising livestock for meat and milk uses enormous amount of energy, food, and water to produce a comparatively small amount of animal-based food. This is a recipe for environmental disaster. Choosing a vegan diet is a powerful and healthy way to rectify this problem and heal our planet— and the transition to veganism may not be as challenging as you might think. It can be a gradual process of eliminating one animal product from your diet at a time. With each change you make to your meal plan, you will not only become healthier but also more compassionate towards animals and aware of the fragile environment around you.

Try it and see.

❑ **Lacto Vegetarian.** Consumes nuts, grains, legumes, seeds, fruit, vegetables, and dairy products, but no other animal product of any kind.

❑ **Lacto-Ovo Vegetarian.** Consumes nuts, grains, legumes, seeds, fruit, vegetables, dairy products, and eggs, but no other animal product of any kind.

❑ **Pescetarian.** Consumes nuts, grains, legumes, seeds, fruit, vegetables, and fish, but no other animal product of any kind.

❑ **Vegan.** Consumes only nuts, grains, legumes, seeds, fruit, vegetables, and herbs. Vegans do not eat honey, dairy products, or any food derived from or containing animal products. Many vegans also refrain from using leather or other animal products as clothing.

❑ **Raw Food Vegan.** Consumes only nuts, legumes, seeds, fruits, vegetables, and herbs, all in uncooked form. Like regular vegans, most raw food vegans avoid using leather and other animal products.

"You eat right, you play right."
—DAVID BECKHAM,
SOCCER PLAYER

As you can see, there is quite a variety of vegetarian practices from which to choose. More and more people, especially teenagers, are adopting a vegetarian lifestyle. While this trend is a good one, we would like to caution parents of vegetarian children: Junk foods such as doughnuts and

Twinkies are not substitutes for animal products! Growing children require protein, which can be found in non-animal sources such as tofu, beans, sprouted grains, and nuts. They also need the nutrients found in vegetables and fruit. These rules apply to adults as well, but it is especially important for teenagers, who have a tendency to skip meals and make unwise food choices that can lead to an unbalanced vegetarian diet. If you want to support their vegetarianism, we suggest that both they and you do some research to see what an appropriate vegetarian eating lifestyle looks like.

A FEW WORDS ABOUT OIL

Oil is highly sensitive to processing. As such, it is very important to be aware of the way commonly used oils are

processed. In their natural state, many oils are rich in proteins and contain highly beneficial omega-3 fatty acids, which stimulate the formation of prostaglandins that, in turn, help control reproduction, inflammation, immune response, and communication between cells. They also prevent blood clots. These benefits, however, are decreased by extraction methods that employ heat and other means of refinement. Even storing oil in a clear bottle can affect its quality, which is diminished by exposure to light. Cold-pressed oil is the most natural and healthy, since no heat is used in its production, allowing it to retain more of its inherent nutrients and flavor. This form of oil is typically more expensive, however, because less oil is obtained using this process.

We usually use organic extra virgin olive oil, macadamia nut oil, coconut oil, or grape seed oil. Sometimes we use more exotic oils such as pumpkin seed oil, walnut oil, and hemp oil. Because these oils are more delicate, they should only be used cold, drizzled over a salad or steamed vegetables.

A FEW WORDS ABOUT NUTS

For years, health experts said that nuts should be rarely eaten because of their high fat content and calorie count. Few knew the true health benefits that lay inside these wonderful substances. The fact is that the fats found in nuts are

monounsaturated and polyunsaturated, which are considered good fats. These substances can actually help prevent heart disease and reduce levels of LDL, the so-called "bad" cholesterol. In addition, according to a study conducted by the Harvard School of Public Health, women who eat nuts or peanut butter five times a week or more significantly lower their risk of type 2 diabetes compared with those who never or rarely consume nuts or peanut butter. (It is important to note that peanuts are technically a legume.)

We do not recommend roasting nuts. We also strongly advise against purchasing peanut butter with added ingredients such as hydrogenated oil. Additionally, it is best to refrigerate all of your nuts, which keeps them fresher and prevents them from going rancid. In fact, try to purchase your nuts already refrigerated. If this is not possible, be sure to purchase nuts already in packages. Just as it is essential to soak grains and beans for optimal digestion, nuts and seeds are best soaked overnight in steam-distilled water to eliminate natural enzyme inhibitors. Once nuts and seeds are soaked, pour off the water, rinse, and store them in a covered glass container in the fridge. They generally keep for two to three days, so it's best to soak only the amount you feel you will consume over such a period of time.

To benefit from all the important nutrients found in nuts, buy them raw, keep them refrigerated, and soak them in pure water—preferably overnight—before eating.

CONCLUSION

Understanding why living foods are so important takes time. It requires you to unlearn what you've blindly regarded as fact for many years. Most people—even in the medical profession—will attest to the fact that the less we cook our foods, the more vitamins, minerals, and especially enzymes are preserved. Jay and I have undergone many years of evolution to arrive at the living foods lifestyle we've come to value. Changing your eating habits is a very personal journey. By sharing what we know to be true about living foods, we hope to shorten your evolution towards more enlightened food choices. In the next chapter, you will learn how to organize your kitchen in a way that will help you easily embrace and maintain this new lifestyle.

5.

Our Living Kitchen

A s you already know, the true path to vital health is a diet high in living foods. But what you may not realize is the central role your kitchen plays in making this lifestyle as easy, stress-free, and enjoyable as possible. Due in large part to busy schedules and the convenience of packaged and processed food, the kitchen is no longer the central space that it once was in most homes. In fact, for many people, "kitchen" has a negative connotation, as it is often associated with chores—particularly the burden of meal preparation and cleanup.

Adopting a wholesome living foods diet—which involves minimal food preparation—removes much of the stress. And the way to make the most of your new lifestyle is to modify your kitchen so that it supports your effort to be truly "living." When the physical elements of your kitchen promote Mother Nature's foods, your perception of your kitchen will be greatly transformed. This is the heart of our "living kitchen" philosophy. In this chapter, we break down the process of creating a living kitchen, from cleaning harmful food and equipment out of your current kitchen and acquiring life-supporting appliances, to shopping for groceries and storing food properly. Following our simple guidelines will put you in a much better position to stick to the living foods program and forever change your relationship with your kitchen.

A living kitchen is essential to making your healthy new lifestyle as easy, stress-free, and truly enjoyable as possible.

OUR "LIVING KITCHEN" PHILOSOPHY

How comfortable do you feel in your kitchen? Do you feel happy, empowered, and in control of your and your family's nutritional needs? If you're like most people, you may find food preparation to be an overwhelming, stressful task. More than ever before, there is pressure to create meals that are not only quick and easy to make, but also healthy and nutritionally balanced. This pressure has given rise to a dysfunctional relationship with eating that supports food manufacturers rather than your ability to nourish yourself and your family. It has also made many people think of their kitchen as a place of drudgery where food is hectically prepared, usually by defrosting, microwaving, or grilling.

Changing your perspective on your kitchen is the key to transforming how and what you eat. Our kitchen is a place of comfort, energy, and enjoyment; a sanctuary that connects us to Nature; and a place in which we can work towards vital health. When you feel at home in your kitchen, food preparation and consumption become a relaxing, pleasurable experience, in turn promoting better food choices and eating habits. And when your kitchen is perfectly equipped for a primarily living foods diet, you can adopt this empowering lifestyle more effortlessly. This is what it means to have a "living kitchen"—a space that completely supports a diet of natural foods to boost your health and happiness. Even your relationship with your family members will begin to change for the better as you invite your children and your spouse or partner to help you in the kitchen. Teaching your children is *vital* to preparing them for a healthy future. A living kitchen—along with vegetable and fruit gardening, discussed in the inset on page 64—brings Nature into your home in an all-encompassing way.

Ultimately, creating a living kitchen is about simplicity. It means eliminating all unnecessary utensils, cookware, and other kitchen supplies that may detract from your new healthy lifestyle, and displaying on the countertops only appliances that promote a living foods diet. Setting up a living kitchen also means getting rid of all processed foods filled with refined sugars, artificial sweeteners, preserva-

Creating a living kitchen is about simplicity. Eliminate unnecessary and potentially harmful appliances, cookware, and foods, and include only those tools and ingredients that promote a healthy diet.

The Power of Gardening

In addition to setting up your living kitchen, maintaining a garden is a great way to enrich your eating experience. Gardening has been part of our lives since Jay and I were children, as we were both raised by families who cultivated lush and inspiring gardens year-round. Back then, it was fairly uncommon for Americans to grow most of their own food, but for our families, it was the norm, as well as a ritual that made us feel empowered and connected to Nature. Growing, picking, and preparing ripe fruits and vegetables—including apples, peaches, apricots, and nectarines—was part of our daily lives, and played a major role in shaping our attitudes towards food at a very early age.

Jay and I highly recommend planting an herb and vegetable garden, as we continue to do today, even if it's just a few plants in your backyard. If possible, add a fruit tree or two. If you live in an apartment, you can still grow sprouts in glass jars or keep pots of herbs on your windowsill. As your plants thrive, so will your relationship to food and Nature, in turn enhancing your living kitchen experience. In addition, the money you spend on produce can shrink by as much as 90 percent, especially if you freeze your home-grown vegetables for future meals and juices. So find a mentor, talk to a neighbor, take a class, or buy a book on organic gardening, and get ready to be inspired.

tives, hydrogenated oils, and other additives. It means stocking up on simple foods that come straight from Nature. Life is much easier and free of stress when you eat natural foods prepared in a kitchen that promotes a living foods lifestyle.

CREATING YOUR LIVING KITCHEN

Take a look around your kitchen. What foods are inside your pantry and refrigerator? What appliances line your countertops? What kinds of cookware and utensils do you keep in your cabinets and drawers? Like most people, your shelves probably contain canned, packaged, and processed foods; sugary cereals and sodas; and snack foods laced with hydrogenated oils. It's also likely that you own a coffee maker, microwave oven, electric can opener, and cooking supplies made of aluminum or coated in Teflon.

Now it's time to get rid of them all. To create your own living kitchen, the commonly owned items listed above must be replaced with foods, appliances, and other implements that support a living foods diet. When you equip your kitchen with only the essentials and organize them so that everything you need is right at your fingertips, you will be in a much better position to both maintain and enjoy your healthy new life.

Creating your living foods kitchen is a multi-step process, and we encourage you to make it as enjoyable as possible. Wear comfortable clothes and put on relaxing, inspirational music. Even though completing this project may require several hours of work, it's worth it. When all is said and done, you will feel enlivened by the new energy present in your kitchen. Just take it one step at a time, and recruit the help of your spouse, children, or friends if you need assistance. Kids may balk at the idea at first, but trust me—they will ultimately appreciate the experience.

Enjoy the process of creating your living foods kitchen. Wear comfortable clothes and listen to music that will both relax and inspire you.

1. Assess Your Kitchen Appliances and Tools

The first step of your total kitchen overhaul involves evaluating each item in your kitchen. Ask yourself if your utensils, cookware, bakeware, appliances, and other supplies support a living foods diet or undermine your ability to become healthier. Whether you realize it or not, there are many common kitchen tools that actually pose health risks. Utensils coated in Teflon—a slippery synthetic substance—and cookware made from aluminum, for example, may contribute to kidney stone formation and even Alzheimer's disease. Provided below is a list of items that interfere with the living foods lifestyle and may be harmful to your health. If you own any of these supplies, we recommend getting rid of them.

> All appliances, cookware, and dishes that contain aluminum, lead, or nonstick surfaces should be removed from your living kitchen.

- ❏ Aluminum cookware and bakeware
- ❏ Coffee makers
- ❏ Copper cookware and bakeware
- ❏ Deep-fat fryers
- ❏ Dishes and glassware containing lead
- ❏ Grills of all kinds
- ❏ Microwave ovens
- ❏ Nonstick cookware and bakeware
- ❏ Plastic containers, dishes, or utensils
- ❏ Roasters
- ❏ Rotisserie ovens
- ❏ Teflon-coated cookware, bakeware, and utensils

Once you have removed these items from your kitchen, it's time to purchase appliances that support a diet of raw foods. The following supplies are listed in order of importance so that you can add them to your kitchen gradually, in case you are on a budget.

Tools and Appliances for Your Living Kitchen

❏ High-powered professional juicer

❏ Professional blender

❏ Stainless steel cookware, preferably waterless

❏ Salad spinner

❏ Dehydrator (not to exceed 115°F, or 46°C)

❏ Automatic sprouter

❏ Automatic grain cooker (stainless steel only)

❏ Stainless steel steamer basket

❏ Professional-grade knives

❏ Paring knives

❏ Saladacco spiralizer (spiral slicer)

❏ Food processor

❏ Hand-held blender

❏ Wheatgrass juicer (stainless steel only)

❏ Water purifier (either steam distiller or reverse osmosis system)

❏ Nut and seed grinder

❏ Nut and seed milk maker

❏ Tofu maker

❏ Pressure cooker

❏ Glass containers for storing foods and juices

❏ Boerner slicer or stainless steel mandoline

❏ Electric teapot

❏ Stainless steel thermoses (at least two)

❏ Half-gallon glass container for sun tea

Our dehydrator.

Our spiralizer (left), slicer (center back), and salad spinner (right).

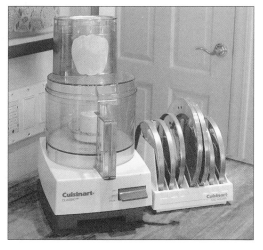

Our food processor.

The Highly Nutritious Coconut

When you read our Living Foods Shopping List, which begins on page 71, you may notice that several coconut products—regular and baby coconuts and coconut oil—are included. A number of recipes in Part Three use coconuts, as well. Although this sweet tropical treat is delicious and has a wonderful texture that enhances many dishes, we have made it a part of our living foods diet not just because we love it, but also because it's one of the most nutritious, healing fruits on Earth.

What health benefits are offered by the delicious coconut? Here are just a few:

☐ Believe it or not, the naturally occurring saturated fats found in coconut oil are *good* for you. Very different from the saturated fats found in meat and dairy, these fats protect heart health, boost metabolism, and help your body burn stored fat for energy.

☐ Fresh coconut is a wonderful source of dietary fiber, with one cup of shredded meat yielding about 7 grams. The fiber satisfies hunger, preventing overeating; normalizes bowel function; prevents blood sugar swings; lowers blood pressure; and reduces the amount of LDL cholesterol ("bad" cholesterol) in the bloodstream.

☐ A serving of fresh coconut provides a bounty of important minerals. Just one cup of this yummy fruit gives you 60 percent of your recommended daily intake of manganese as well as significant amounts of copper, selenium, potassium, iron, phosphorus, magnesium, and zinc. Combined, these nutrients help maintain normal body functions.

☐ Fresh coconuts offer a wealth of vitamins. For instance, they are very high in vitamin C, which helps protect the health of your blood vessels, muscles, bones, and connective tissue. Coconut also provides substantial amounts of vitamins B_1 (thiamin), B_2 (riboflavin), and B_3 (niacin).

☐ Coconuts contain *lauric acid*, which is a natural anti-bacterial and anti-viral agent. By eating the meat and drinking the milk of this fruit, you will bolster your body's immune system and help it fight off infection.

If coconuts are new to you, you'll want to turn to page 91, where you'll find an inset that guides you through choosing and using baby coconuts—our favorite form of this fabulous food. Enjoy!

As you adopt a living foods lifestyle and use the recipes presented in Part Three, you may become aware of additional equipment that would be helpful in your living kitchen. Just be sure to stick to healthy materials, like stainless steel, and you will find your new lifestyle increasingly enjoyable as you get the tools you need to make food preparation easy.

2. Consider Your Foods Carefully

A well-equipped kitchen is useless if doesn't contain the right foods. But before you can fill your kitchen with fresh fruits, vegetables, grains, and other raw fare, it's wise to remove the unhealthy products that clutter your shelves. Cleaning out your pantry and refrigerator is an opportunity to become more mindful of the kinds of nourishing foods that you really want and need in your kitchen. Here are some products and ingredients that are important to eliminate from your kitchen as well as your life in general:

❏ Alcohol of any kind, including wines that contain sulfur dioxide or are made from non-organic grapes

❏ Artificial sweeteners

❏ Breads containing dough conditioners, calcium prionate, mono-diglycerides, and yeast. (Brewer's yeast is acceptable.)

❏ Coffee, including decaf

❏ Dairy products

❏ Deli meats that contain nitrates and nitrites

❏ Foods containing artificial colors and flavorings

❏ Foods containing hydrogenated or partially hydrogenated oils, which are found in margarine, most commercial snack foods (chips, crackers, cookies, muffins, cakes, pies, candy bars, etc.), and many cereals and coffee creamers

❏ Heat-extracted oils, including cotton seed oil, safflower oil, corn oil, and peanut oil

TIP

Avoid putting fresh fruit or hot foods in plastic containers. These foods can cause harmful chemicals to leach out of the plastic and into what you eat. We recommend using lidded glass containers and stainless steel thermoses, which are far more sterile and functional than plastic.

❏ Soft drinks of any kind, including so-called natural beverages

❏ White-flour and white-sugar products

❏ White rice, including white basmati rice

It's also wise to eliminate all canned foods and packaged items—including herbs and spices—that have not been used in a year or more. Once these unhealthy items are removed from your kitchen, it's time to stock up on foods that fit your new lifestyle. On page 71, you'll find a comprehensive shopping list that includes produce, beverages, and other essential ingredients. Most of the items are used in the recipes found in Part Three, which maximize the nutritional value and taste of each food and ingredient. Wherever you do your shopping, be sure to buy only organic all-natural foods, whether fresh or packaged. Although the majority (at least 50 to 75 percent) of your diet should be comprised of living foods, some packaged items are acceptable and are included in the list. However, use these foods sparingly, and buy only products that are sold in glass bottles, not plastic containers. Oils should be unrefined and extracted mechanically—not with chemicals or high heat. Nuts should be raw—not roasted. Grains and grain products should be whole, not refined. Condiments like tamari should be made without artificial ingredients—and without gluten, as well, if you're following a gluten-free lifestyle. Dried fruits should be grown organically and dried without the addition of sulfites. Tofu should be non-GMO (non-genetically modified organism) and organic. In sum, every food and ingredient you buy should be produced organically and as close as possible to its natural state.

In addition to the sprouts on the following list, we also recommend sprouting adzuki beans, barley, garbanzo beans, fenugreek, sunflower seeds, triticale, and wheat berries, among many other foods. See the inset on page 102 of Part Three for sprouting instructions.

To keep your herbs and spices as fresh and flavorful as possible, store them in a drawer, away from light and heat.

Our Living Foods Shopping List

Breads, Cereals, and Grains

- ☐ Brown rice, long-grain and short-grain
- ☐ Buckwheat (soba) noodles
- ☐ Bulgur wheat
- ☐ Couscous (regular or gluten-free)
- ☐ Millet
- ☐ Oats, steel-cut and rolled (regular or gluten-free)
- ☐ Pearl barley
- ☐ Pita, whole-grain
- ☐ Quinoa
- ☐ Tortillas (basil, corn, and spinach)
- ☐ Triticale
- ☐ Wheat berries
- ☐ Wild rice

Fruits

- ☐ Acai berries
- ☐ Apples, such as Fuji, Golden Delicious, Red Delicious, and Pippin
- ☐ Apricots, fresh and dried
- ☐ Avocados, preferably Haas
- ☐ Bananas, red and yellow
- ☐ Blackberries
- ☐ Blueberries
- ☐ Boysenberries
- ☐ Cantaloupes
- ☐ Casaba melons
- ☐ Cherries, fresh and dried
- ☐ Coconuts, fresh, baby and regular
- ☐ Coconuts, dried, unsweetened
- ☐ Cranberries, fresh and dried
- ☐ Dates, fresh and dried
- ☐ Figs, fresh and dried
- ☐ Gooseberries
- ☐ Grapefruit
- ☐ Grapes (red, green, Ribier, and Concord)
- ☐ Honeydew melons
- ☐ Kiwis
- ☐ Lemons
- ☐ Limes
- ☐ Mangos
- ☐ Nectarines
- ☐ Olives, black and green
- ☐ Oranges, navel (for eating) and Valencia (for juicing)
- ☐ Papayas
- ☐ Peaches
- ☐ Pears
- ☐ Pineapples
- ☐ Plums, fresh and dried
- ☐ Pomegranates
- ☐ Raisins
- ☐ Raspberries
- ☐ Star fruit (carambola)
- ☐ Strawberries
- ☐ Tangelos
- ☐ Tangerines
- ☐ Tomatoes (vine-ripened plum, cherry, Roma, or heirloom)
- ☐ Watermelon

Herbs, Spices, and Flavorings		
☐ Anise	☐ Clove	☐ Parsley, fresh
☐ Basil	☐ Cumin	☐ Peppermint
☐ Bay leaves	☐ Curry powder	☐ Red pepper, crushed
☐ Bernard Jensen's Vegetable Seasoning Blend	☐ Dill weed, fresh	☐ Rosemary
	☐ Fennel	☐ Sage
☐ Black pepper	☐ Garlic	☐ Sea salt, preferably Celtic
☐ Burdock root	☐ Ginger	
☐ Cajun seasoning blend	☐ Herbes de Provence	☐ Spearmint
☐ Cayenne pepper	☐ Italian seasoning blend	☐ Spike seasoning blend
☐ Celery salt	☐ Marjoram	☐ Tarragon
☐ Chives	☐ Nutmeg	☐ Thyme
☐ Cilantro, fresh	☐ Oregano	☐ Vanilla extract (pure)
☐ Cinnamon	☐ Paprika	☐ White pepper

Legumes		
☐ Adzuki beans	☐ Garbanzo beans (chickpeas)	☐ Mung beans
☐ Black beans		☐ Pinto beans
☐ Black-eyed peas	☐ Kidney beans	☐ White navy beans
	☐ Lentils (French, green, red, and/or yellow)	

Nuts and Seeds		
☐ Almonds	☐ Macadamia nuts	☐ Pumpkin seeds
☐ Cashews	☐ Peanuts	☐ Sesame seeds
☐ Filberts	☐ Pecans	☐ Sunflower seeds
☐ Flax seeds	☐ Pine nuts	☐ Walnuts
☐ Hemp seeds	☐ Pomegranate seeds	

Oils		
☐ Borage oil	☐ Hemp oil	☐ Pumpkin seed oil
☐ Coconut oil	☐ Macadamia nut oil	☐ Sesame oil
☐ Flaxseed oil	☐ Olive oil, extra virgin	☐ Walnut oil
☐ Grape seed oil		

Specialty Foods, Superfoods, and Supplements

- ☐ Acidophilus, liquid or powdered
- ☐ Bee pollen
- ☐ Blackstrap molasses
- ☐ Bragg Liquid Aminos
- ☐ Capers
- ☐ Carob powder
- ☐ Edamame (fresh soybeans)
- ☐ Green barley
- ☐ Green tea soba noodles
- ☐ Kelp powder
- ☐ Kombu
- ☐ Liquid chlorophyll
- ☐ Miso, brown and white
- ☐ Nori
- ☐ Nutritional yeast
- ☐ Powdered enzymes
- ☐ Powdered vitamin C
- ☐ Purslane
- ☐ Sesame tahini
- ☐ Spirulina
- ☐ Sun-dried tomatoes
- ☐ Super green powder supplement
- ☐ Tamari (regular or gluten-free)
- ☐ Tofu (firm, extra firm, and silken)
- ☐ Tofu, sprouted (firm only)
- ☐ Vegetable bouillon cubes
- ☐ Wheatgrass

Sprouts	☐ Alfalfa	☐ Broccoli	☐ Mung bean

Teas	☐ Chamomile	☐ Ginger	☐ Peppermint
	☐ Dandelion	☐ Ginseng	☐ Spearmint
	☐ Echinacea		

Vegetables	☐ Anaheim peppers	☐ Collard greens	☐ Peas
	☐ Artichokes, all types	☐ Corn	☐ Potatoes (brown, red, white, or yellow)
	☐ Arugula	☐ Cucumbers	
	☐ Asparagus	☐ Dandelion greens	☐ Pumpkin
	☐ Baby field greens (mixed)	☐ Endive	☐ Radicchio
		☐ Fennel	☐ Radishes
	☐ Beet greens	☐ Fenugreek	☐ Scallions (green onions)
	☐ Beets	☐ Green beans	☐ Shallots
	☐ Bell peppers (green, orange, red, and yellow)	☐ Jalapeño peppers	☐ Spinach
		☐ Jicama	☐ Squash (acorn, banana, butternut, Kaboca, summer, turban)
	☐ Bok choy (Chinese cabbage)	☐ Kale	
		☐ Leeks	
	☐ Broccoli	☐ Lettuce (butter, red-leaf, or romaine)	☐ String beans
	☐ Brussels sprouts		☐ Sweet potatoes
	☐ Cabbage (green, napa, and red)	☐ Mushrooms (oyster and shiitake)	☐ Swiss chard (green, red, and/or rainbow)
	☐ Carrots	☐ Onions (red, yellow, sweet, or sprouted)	☐ Turnip greens
	☐ Cauliflower		☐ Turnips
	☐ Celery	☐ Pea shoots	☐ Watercress
			☐ Zucchini

Condiments and Other Prepared Ingredients	☐ Apple cider vinegar	☐ Mustard, Dijon and other styles	☐ Peanut butter, nonhydrogenated
	☐ Balsamic vinegar	☐ Natural sweeteners, like agave nectar, coconut sugar, date sugar, honey, and stevia	☐ Relish
	☐ Chili paste		☐ Rice milk
	☐ Egg-free mayonnaise, such as Nayonaise		☐ Rice vinegar
	☐ Ketchup	☐ Nut butters, like almond or cashew	☐ Soy milk
	☐ Maple syrup		☐ Thai peanut sauce

3. Establish a System

A common misconception about the living foods diet is that it requires a great deal of work and preparation, which most people try to avoid at all costs. Yet, eating and preparing living foods is actually far easier, simpler, and more convenient than following a diet of cooked foods. Plus, once you find a routine that works for you, grocery shopping and meal preparation are a breeze. Years ago, Jay and I developed a system of food shopping, washing, and storing that has worked well for us for several decades. Our step-by-step guidelines, presented below, will save you time and energy, as well as motivate you to eat right.

1. **Buy groceries only twice a week.** We divide our grocery shopping between two days, Wednesday and Friday. On Fridays, we purchase most of the foods that we'll need for the next several days from a local grocery store that has a big selection of organic foods. (Another good source would be a health food store that carries produce or a supermarket with an organic produce section.) We always buy a twenty-five-pound bag of organic horse carrots—which costs only about five dollars—as well as a sufficient supply of apples, avoca-

By purchasing groceries twice a week, you will help ensure a ready supply of fresh fruits and vegetables, as well as staples like olive oil, flax seeds, and nuts.

If You Can't Have Gluten

Throughout this chapter, we recommend a long list of foods that are healthy for most people. If you have any dietary allergies or intolerances, however, you know that you have to be very careful in your selection of foods. One intolerance of which people are now becoming increasingly aware is *gluten intolerance*, also known as *celiac disease*.

Gluten is a protein found in wheat, barley, rye, and triticale (a cross between wheat and rye). It is also found in foods that are derived from these grains—in wheat-based soy sauce, for instance—and sometimes in oats. People who have celiac disease can experience a range of disabling symptoms, including chronic diarrhea and weight loss, when they eat even small amounts of gluten.

The vast majority of the foods used in this book are naturally gluten-free. All vegetables and fruits, for instance, do not include this protein. But both Our Living Foods Shopping List (see page 71) and some of our recipes include grains and pastas that have gluten, and some recipes use bread, which, in most cases, includes gluten. If you are gluten-intolerant, we suggest that you explore the many grains that do not contain this protein. Millet, quinoa, gluten-free couscous (made with rice), and brown rice are four great options. Also look for special breads, pastas, seasonings, and other products that specifically say "Gluten Free" on the label. To help you benefit from a wide variety of healthy living dishes, for every recipe that contains a "problem" food such as bulgur wheat, we suggest an alternative gluten-free product in the "For a Change" section at the end of the recipe. This means that, with occasional adjustments, you can enjoy virtually every recipe in this book!

dos, fresh vegetables and fruits, grains, and staples like olive oil, flax oil, flax seeds, and nuts. On Wednesdays, we go to a nearby farmer's market, where we buy organic greens for salads, as well as about four different kinds of seasonal fruits and vegetables. Splitting up your grocery shopping in this way will allow you to always have a supply of fresh ripe foods ready and waiting to be eaten.

2. **Wash produce.** Clean most fruits and vegetables as soon as you get home from the grocery store—while you are still motivated—in order to save time later during the meal preparation process. This is one of our keys to maintaining a living food diet. It's best to wash produce like apples, plums, and tomatoes thoroughly and to soak them for a few

minutes or make sure that all contaminants are removed. More "delicate" produce such as berries, peaches, and kiwi should be washed directly before eating or juicing. If you are unable to buy organic produce, be sure to use a pesticide-removal wash. (Check our website—listed on page 211—for a great product that we developed.) Rinse all fruits and vegetables after using any pesticide wash.

3. Spin-dry greens. Since even the smallest amount of water can quickly turn leaves brown and mushy, a salad spinner is a kitchen essential. Always spin-dry greens like parsley, cilantro, and spinach after washing to keep them fresh. If you are pressed for time, you can buy bagged organic baby field greens, which come pre-washed and last up to four days after opening. These greens can be expensive, though, so when you have the time, we recommend buying and washing a variety of organic lettuces, and storing them in plastic bags in the refrigerator. Place a paper towel in each bag to absorb any moisture and prevent the greens from getting slimy.

Wash and dry most of your fruits and vegetables as soon as you get them home from the supermarket, grocery store, or farmer's market. This step is key to making meal preparation fast and easy.

4. Carefully store your food. Place most of the vegetables in the refrigerator to preserve their freshness. Try to keep them organized so that they can be easily found when it comes time to juice or prepare a meal. After trimming the carrots, we like to store them in bins at the bottom of the refrigerator in order to reserve shelf space for bags of washed greens and other veggies, as well as oils and nuts, which can go rancid quickly when left unrefrigerated. The shelves are also good for holding sprouted grains, soaked nuts, spreads, freshly made nut milk—all of which should be kept in glass containers—and a few bottled food items. The only fruits you should store in the refrigerator are apples and berries, which should be wrapped in a paper towel and placed in an airtight glass container. Other fruits can be left out in bowls on your countertops, as this will allow them to ripen more quickly and enhance their flavor. Finally, the pantry is a good area for ingredients like dried herbs and spices, which must be kept in a cool dark place to preserve taste and quality. Vegetables that do not require refrigeration, such as onions and potatoes, can also be stored in the pantry, along with grains, pastas, and other nonperishables.

From start to finish, the process of washing, drying, and storing your food should take only an hour or so. If time allows, you can cook several days' worth of organic grains, such as brown rice, in a stainless steel rice cooker. Be sure to soak your grains overnight or for at least an hour before cooking. This enhances their enzymatic activity, thereby improving digestion. If some vegetables from your last shopping trip are still in the fridge, you may also want to prepare a soup. (See page 130 for "Living Soups" and page 140 for "Cooked Choices" soups.) In the winter, you can incorporate more cooked grains and soups into your eating regimen, but they should account for only about 25 percent of your diet.

Contrary to popular belief, eating natural uncooked foods is neither complex nor time-consuming. And when you fol-

---

TIP

Do not store fruits in close proximity to vegetables. Most fruits emit a natural gas called ethylene, which causes fruits and veggies to ripen more quickly. So if you want your produce to stay fresh, be sure to separate it. Bananas in particular are a significant source of ethylene, so you may want to purchase a banana hanger to keep them away from other fruits.

low our system, most meals should take only about ten to fifteen minutes to prepare, making the experience easy and fun. Now, at any time, you will be ready to enjoy a fresh living juice or meal stress-free.

CONCLUSION

While it's easy for us to describe the concrete details of our living kitchen, it's more difficult to convey its non-physical benefits. Establishing a space in your home that is truly "living" will enhance not only your body, but also your spiritual, mental, and emotional health. Filling it with the proper foods and appliances is only part of the transformation; you can also create a calming atmosphere by lighting candles, playing soothing music, growing plants and herbs, and decorating the walls with pictures of your loved ones. When you embrace your kitchen as your sanctuary, food preparation is a gratifying experience that unites family and friends. So now that you have all the necessary information, tools, and ingredients, it's time to put it all together and begin making dishes that are equally satisfying and health-sustaining.

"Simple foods are power foods"

—JAY KORDICH

PART THREE

Our Living Recipes

In the following pages, we share some of the recipes we have been creating together for well over thirty years. Our juicing and smoothie recipes are the best you can find anywhere, and many are designed to help the body heal itself of degenerative diseases, including toxemia. Our other recipes—including salads, soups, spreads, breakfast dishes, and more—round out your diet so that you can enjoy a variety of delicious living foods.

Part Three begins with what we call our "basic" recipes. Designed for people who are just starting a living foods diet, this section includes fundamental dishes like Basic Julienned Veggie Salad (page 86) and Basic Oatmeal (page 95). Usually, when people are making the transition to natural foods, they start with the "basics" and, over time, move on to other dishes. But for the healthiest transition, we recommend that you base the way you start your living foods diet on the test provided on page 52 of Chapter 4. Your answers will enable you to determine the percentage of your transition diet that should be composed of living foods. If, up to this point, you have eaten mostly cooked foods, you should begin with a diet that's approximately 50 percent living and gradually incorporate more living foods into your daily menus. We have made this easy by clearly marking each recipe with the percentage of the dish that is living. For instance, our Basic Julienned Veggie Salad is "100% Living," while our Basic Oatmeal is "25% Living" because the oatmeal is cooked. Ultimately, you'll want to aim for a diet that's at least 75 percent living.

GET READY!

Before you make your first recipe, we suggest that you read Chapter 5, "Our Living Kitchen." There, you'll find a list of the foods we use in our own kitchen (see page 71 including vegetables, fruits, grains, beans, oils, vinegars, and more. This will help you stock your kitchen so that you have all the ingredients you need to get started. In the same chapter, you will find a list of tools and appliances we use to make our living foods recipes (see page 67).

Finally, check out pages 75 to 78 to learn about the advance preparation that will allow you to get in and out of the kitchen quickly and still enjoy a delicious, healthy meal. On our program, you will spend an hour or so, one or two days a week—whatever days you have off—washing and storing greens, vegetables, and fruits. You can also prepare a whole grain that you can include in your dishes for the next few days, and, if time permits, you can cook several servings of soup.

Once you've done your grocery shopping and food prep, you can go out to eat that evening without feeling guilty. You have prepared healthy, vital, energy-boosting foods that will last you for days. Imagine all the money you'll save by preparing a large amount of soup for a few dollars, instead of one cup for $3.50 or more! The amount manufacturers charge for a small portion of soup is just outrageous. The prices are sky high for frozen foods, canned beans, and packaged cereals, as well. You can save a great deal of money by buying fresh, unprocessed foods as often as possible.

Interestingly, most people think that healthy foods are difficult to find, but you'll probably find this true of only one of our favorite ingredients—baby coconuts. If your regular grocery store does not have them, you will probably be able to find them very easily in an Asian grocery store. Bring your young children, teenagers, or grandchildren along with you so that you can all learn together how another culture eats. It's sure to expand your horizons. If you don't want to venture out into an Asian market, ask someone at your local grocery or health food store to special-order these exotic treats for you.

CREATING A HEALTHIER FUTURE

We ask that you give yourself and your family the time you need to make the transition to a new diet. Realize, too, that when you adopt a healthier diet, you help make the world a healthier place. The more you improve your eating habits, the more the food manufacturers and restaurateurs will change in response to you. Back in 1964, when I was a little girl, my family had to go to Chinese restaurants or Seventh Day Adventist cafeterias to get vegetarian foods. Now there are more and more juice bars (thanks to Jay!) and vegetarian restaurant choices. If we keep this up, we will create a far better future for ourselves and future generations.

We are not sure if you realize just how unhealthy we are as a nation. Ironically, we are one of the world's richest nations, yet we are nearly at the bottom of the list of the world's healthiest countries. The two of us attribute this to stressful lifestyles, demanding jobs, and poor-quality foods. The American diet is too high in animal products, sugary processed foods, and canned foods, as well as the high-fat nutrition-poor foods sold at fast food restaurants.

How can you improve your own diet and your own health? Begin by eating at home. Start creating a rich life for yourself and your family right in your own kitchen, and good health will follow. The recipes presented in this section of the book will help you begin your journey to wellness.

Our Natural Food Pyramid

Our Natural Food Pyramid illustrates the best living food choices for your diet. The base of the pyramid—fresh veggie juices, pure water, raw veggies, and raw fruits—should form the greatest part of your diet. You should be consuming at least 5 pounds of salad per week, with these salads including not only raw produce, but also tofu, beans, grains, and other nutritious additions. As you move up the pyramid, you'll find foods, such as raisins, that should be eaten less frequently—perhaps only once or twice a week. Natural sweeteners, such as honey and coconut sugar, should be consumed not only infrequently, but also sparingly.

For information on acceptable foods in each of the following categories, see the table of foods used in our living kitchen on pages 71 to 74 of Chapter 5.

Pure Oils, Yeast-Free Breads (weekly)

Dates, Raisins, Stevia, or Other Natural Sweeteners (twice weekly)

Grains, Sprouted Grains, Steamed Vegetables (1 serving per day)

Beans, Fresh Fruit Juices, Tempeh, Tofu, Sprouted Tofu (1 serving per day)

Nuts, Seeds, Sprouts, Superfoods (2 serving per day)

All Raw Veggies, Raw Greens, Fresh Fruits (3–5 servings per day)

Fresh Veggie Juices (32 ounces per day)
Pure Water (64 ounces per day)

Our Basic Salad (see page 85).

Basic Recipes

Our "Basics" are designed to start you on a delicious diet of living foods. In the following pages, you'll find both savory and sweet salads, a unique "spaghetti" entrée, a hot-and hearty breakfast cereal, and even a fantastically fresh living pie. Remember that *simple* foods are *power* foods!

Basic Salad

A wonderful accompaniment to both cooked and living meals, our Basic Salad is easy to prepare and adds a generous amount of living foods to your diet.

1 large head romaine lettuce, cut into bite-sized pieces

1 cup (75 g) bite-sized pieces regular or baby spinach

2 vine-ripened tomatoes, cut into 1-inch chunks

1 cucumber, peeled and sliced

$1/2$ cup (50 g) sliced red onion

Basic Dressing

$1/2$ cup (118 ml) extra virgin olive oil

2 tablespoons tamari or Bragg Liquid Aminos

SERVINGS: 2   100% LIVING

1 To make the dressing, place the olive oil and tamari in a small bowl, and whisk until well-blended and thickened. Set aside.

2 To make the salad, place all of the salad ingredients in a large bowl, and toss to mix.

3 Directly before serving, pour the desired amount of dressing over the salad and toss until the ingredients are well coated. Serve immediately.

FOR A CHANGE

◆ If you have to avoid gluten, be sure to buy a gluten-free brand of tamari or to use Bragg Liquid Aminos, which is gluten-free.

◆ For a refreshing citrus flavor, replace the tamari with $1/4$ cup of fresh lemon or lime juice and one crushed clove of garlic.

Basic Julienned Veggie Salad

This beautiful salad is very versatile. Add the vibrantly colored veggie mixture to our Basic Salad (see page 85), or wrap the dressed veggies in a spinach tortilla.

1 cup (100 g) julienned jicama

1 cup (175 g) julienned zucchini

1 cup (128 g) julienned carrots

1 cup (150 g) julienned beets

Tarragon Dressing

2 tablespoons chopped fresh tarragon

1 tablespoon apple cider vinegar

1 clove garlic

$^1/_2$ cup (118 ml) extra virgin olive oil

Sea salt and black pepper to taste

SERVINGS: 2   **100% LIVING**

1 To make the dressing, place the tarragon, vinegar, and garlic in a blender. Slowly add the oil in a stream while the blender is processing. Season to taste with salt and pepper, and set aside.

2 To make the salad, place all of the vegetables in a large bowl, and toss to mix.

3 Add the dressing to the salad, and toss until the ingredients are well coated. Serve.

Basic Rice Salad

This salad is a healthy, delicious mixture of living foods and cooked whole grains. For a great meal, pair it with a juice that aids digestion, such as Popeye's Digestive Special (see page 168).

3 cups (450 g) shredded carrots

6 scallions (green onions), minced

$2/3$ cup (16 g) minced fresh parsley

4 cups (1 kg) hot cooked brown rice

8 large romaine lettuce leaves, chopped (for garnish)

2 large tomatoes, cut into wedges (for garnish)

$3/4$ cup (100 g) pitted black olives (for garnish)

Lemon Dressing

$1/4$ cup (59 ml) fresh lemon juice

2 tablespoons tamari or Braggs Liquid Aminos

1 tablespoon chopped fresh dill

$1/2$ teaspoon sea salt

$1/4$ teaspoon black pepper

2 tablespoons extra virgin olive oil

SERVINGS: 4   75% LIVING

1 To make the dressing, place the lemon juice in a small bowl and stir in the tamari, dill, salt, and pepper. Slowly whisk in the oil, beating until well blended. Set aside.

2 To make the salad, place the carrots, scallions, and parsley in a large bowl, and stir to mix. Add the rice while it is still hot, and toss. Add the prepared dressing, and toss until the ingredients are well coated.

3 Mound the salad on a serving dish and garnish with the lettuce leaves, tomato wedges, and black olives. Serve.

FOR A CHANGE

◆ For variety, substitute different fresh herbs for those used in the recipe. Cilantro, basil, and thyme are just a few good choices.

◆ To add more living foods to this recipe, toss in julienned raw veggies such as zucchini, bell peppers, jicama, or carrots, and/or steamed broccoli or cauliflower.

◆ If you have to avoid gluten, be sure to buy a gluten-free brand of tamari or to use Bragg Liquid Aminos, which is gluten-free.

Basic Soba Noodle Salad

A fusion of Asian and Italian flavors, this is a wonderfully substantial dish. Look for soba noodles—also called buckwheat noodles—in your local health food store or Asian market. For a complete meal, accompany the salad with our Three "C's" Digestive Juice (see page 169).

1 pound (454 g) green soba noodles, cooked according to package directions

1 head romaine lettuce, cut into bite-sized pieces

1 cup (100 g) thinly sliced napa cabbage

1 cup (120 g) chopped black olives

$^3/_4$ cup (75 g) rings red onion

$^1/_2$ cup (88 g) broccoli florets, steamed

$^1/_2$ cup (90 g) halved green beans, steamed

$^1/_2$ cup (75 g) julienned zucchini

$^1/_2$ cup (75 g) julienned yellow summer squash

$^1/_2$ cup (88 g) diced red bell pepper

1 small tomato, chopped

Basil-Lemon Dressing

$^1/_3$ cup (15 g) chopped fresh basil

$^1/_3$ cup (79 ml) fresh lemon juice

2 tablespoons pine nuts

3 cloves garlic

1 cup (237 ml) extra virgin olive oil

Sea salt and black pepper to taste

SERVINGS: 4   60–75% LIVING

1 To make the dressing, place the basil, lemon juice, pine nuts, and garlic in a blender. Slowly add the oil in a stream while the blender is processing. Season to taste with salt and pepper, and set aside.

2 To make the salad, place all of the salad ingredients in a large bowl, and toss to mix. Add the prepared dressing, and toss until the ingredients are well coated. Serve.

FOR A CHANGE

◆ If you have to avoid gluten, make sure that the soba noodles you buy are marked "gluten-free." Although buckwheat does not contain gluten, some brands of noodles are made with some wheat flour, which means that the product includes some gluten.

◆ For a subtly different texture, substitute baby field greens for the romaine lettuce.

John's Basic Living Spaghetti

This is a great summer dish. Enjoy it with our Basic Salad (page 85) and perhaps some flax crackers.

2 zucchini, julienned or spirilized

2 yellow summer squash, julienned or spirilized

Sauce

6 medium vine-ripened tomatoes

$1/2$ cup (23 g) fresh basil

$1/2$ cup (118 ml) extra virgin olive oil

2 large cloves garlic

1 teaspoon sea salt

$1/2$ teaspoon black pepper

Water

SERVINGS: 2   100% LIVING

1 To make the sauce, place all of the sauce ingredients except for the water in a blender. If you like your sauce chunky, pulse the mixture, adding water as necessary until the sauce reaches the desired consistency. (We usually add about $1/2$ cup water.) If you like your sauce smooth, blend at high speed for about 30 seconds. Set aside.

2 Place the squash "spaghetti" in a bowl. Pour the sauce over the top, toss to coat, and serve.

FOR A CHANGE

◆ For added flavor and crunch, sprinkle pine nuts over the spaghetti before serving.

Basic Living Pie

Our living pies are incredible. There is no added sugar—just fruit, seeds, and some spices. These pies are loaded with healthy fats and proteins, are very digestible, and can be made with a number of different fruits. (See "For a Change" at the end of the recipe.)

Topping

1 baby coconut and its liquid*

1 large mango, peeled and cut into chunks

$^1/_2$ teaspoon vanilla extract

$^1/_2$ teaspoon ground cinnamon, nutmeg, or cloves

1 cup (75 g) shredded unsweetened coconut (for garnish)

Crust

1 $^1/_2$ cups (210 g) sunflower seeds

$^1/_2$ cup (75 g) raisins

8 pitted medjool dates

Filling

1 banana, thinly sliced

1 pear, peeled and thinly sliced

2 apples, peeled and shredded

* See page 91 for preparation instructions.

SERVINGS: 4   **100% LIVING**

1 To make the topping, place the baby coconut meat and liquid, mango chunks, vanilla extract, and cinnamon in a blender, and blend until thick and creamy. (Do *not* include the shredded coconut.) Refrigerate for 1 hour.

2 To prepare the crust, place all of the crust ingredients in a food processor, and blend for about 3 minutes or until the mixture begins to clump.

3 Transfer the crust mixture to an 11-inch pie pan (preferably glass) and press it evenly on the bottom and sides to form a crust. Refrigerate for about 10 minutes.

4 Arrange a layer of banana slices on top of the cooled crust, followed by a layer of pears and a layer of apples. Repeat if necessary.

5 Spoon the chilled topping over the pie. Sprinkle the shredded coconut over the top, and refrigerate for at least 1 hour before serving. Store leftovers in the refrigerator for up to 2 days.

FOR A CHANGE

◆ For a different spin on the Basic Living Pie, replace the fruits in the filling with 2 thinly sliced peaches or nectarines, 10 thinly sliced strawberries, and 15 whole blueberries or 10 whole boysenberries. You'll love the beautiful colors!

Opening Baby Coconuts

Baby coconuts—also sold as *young coconuts, tender coconuts,* or *Thai coconuts*—are cylindrical in shape, about 7 or 8 inches across, and have a cone-shaped top. They are filled with nutrient-rich "milk," and the "meat" inside is tender and silky. Available in natural foods stores, specialty shops, and Asian markets, most baby coconuts have had their outer husks removed, making them white in color and relatively easy to open. Make sure that the baby coconuts you purchase are organic and have not been sprayed with pesticides or other chemicals. You want your coconut to be free of contaminants.

Although there are many different methods for opening these delicious fruits, we recommend the following:

1. Stand the coconut upright and grip it firmly with one hand.

2. Using a sharp knife with a sturdy blade, carefully insert the blade at a slight angle into the coconut about 2 inches from the top. Move the blade from side to side to increase the size of the slit, then remove the knife.

3. Next to the slit, insert the blade again, and repeat the process until you have cut a circle into the top of the coconut and can remove the circular piece.

4. Now you can easily pour out the liquid from within the coconut and spoon out the flesh, which releases easily.

The meat of the coconut should be white, and the liquid should be clear. If the meat or water is pink, it may mean that the fruit is not as fresh as it should be. In that case, it's best to choose another coconut.

Basic Cool-Weather Fruit Salad

This is a great salad to make in the autumn, when so many varieties of pears are available. Use the juiciest pears you can find, and enjoy this dish for breakfast on a beautiful fall morning. It's a wonderful way to start your day.

2 medium pears (unpeeled), cut into 1-inch slices

2 medium apples (unpeeled), thinly sliced

1 banana, sliced

$^1/_3$ cup (42 g) chopped walnuts

$^1/_3$ cup (47 g) sunflower seeds

$^1/_3$ cup (60 g) flax seeds (for garnish)

Dressing

1 baby coconut and its liquid*

$^1/_2$ cup (74 g) macadamia nuts

1-inch piece fresh ginger, peeled

Dash vanilla extract, if desired

Dash honey, agave nectar, coconut sugar, or other natural sweeteners, if desired

* See page 91 for preparation instructions.

SERVINGS: 2   100% LIVING

1 To make the dressing, place the coconut and its liquid in the blender. Add the nuts, ginger, and, if desired, the vanilla extract and honey. Process the dressing ingredients until they have a creamy consistency. Set aside.

2 To make the salad, place all of the salad ingredients except for the flax seeds in a large bowl, and toss to mix.

3 Add the dressing to the salad, and toss until the ingredients are well coated. Sprinkle on the flax seeds, and serve.

FOR A CHANGE

◆ For added sweetness, replace the flax seeds garnish with dark raisins.

Basic Cool-Weather Fruit Salad (see page 92).

Basic Warm-Weather Fruit Salad

If you want to prepare this salad earlier in the day, omit the dressing and squeeze a bit of lemon juice over the top to prevent the apples and other fruits from browning. Under refrigeration, this dish will keep up to twelve hours. Add the dressing just before serving.

2 medium nectarines (unpeeled), sliced

2 peaches, peeled and sliced

2 medium-sized apples (unpeeled), thinly sliced

1 banana, sliced

1 cup (200 g) sliced strawberries

$1/2$ cup (63 g) chopped walnuts

$1/4$ cup (19 g) shredded unsweetened coconut

Dressing

1 baby coconut and its liquid*

$1/2$ cup (74 g) macadamia nuts

1-inch piece fresh ginger, peeled

2 tablespoons coconut sugar, agave nectar, or maple syrup

Dash of vanilla extract, if desired

* See page 91 for preparation instructions.

SERVINGS: 2   100% LIVING

1 To make the dressing, place the coconut and its liquid in the blender. Add the nuts, ginger, sugar or syrup, and, if desired, the vanilla extract. Process the dressing ingredients until they have a creamy consistency. Set aside.

2 To make the salad, place all of the salad ingredients in a large bowl, and toss to mix.

3 Add the dressing to the salad, and toss until the ingredients are well coated. Serve.

Basic Oatmeal

This is a wonderful breakfast on a cool morning—delicious and satisfying. Top it with nuts, fruit, or perhaps a dash of your favorite spice, and enjoy!

2 cups (474 ml) water

1 cup (176 g) uncooked steel-cut oats, soaked for at least 1 hour

$\frac{1}{2}$ teaspoon sea salt

2 tablespoons coconut oil

Dash flax seeds (for garnish)

Optional Additions

$\frac{1}{2}$ cup (75 g) raisins

$\frac{1}{2}$ cup (63 g) chopped walnuts

$\frac{1}{2}$ cup (88 g) chopped dates

$\frac{1}{2}$ cup (63 g) grated apple

$\frac{1}{2}$ cup (80 g) grated pear

$\frac{1}{2}$ teaspoon ground cinnamon

$\frac{1}{4}$ teaspoon ground nutmeg

SERVINGS: 2   **25% LIVING**

1 Place the water in a large saucepan, and bring to a boil over high heat.

2 Drain any excess soaking water from the oats. Stir the oats and salt into the cooking water, and return to a boil, stirring frequently to prevent clumping. Reduce the heat to a simmer and cook, stirring occasionally, for about 30 minutes or until the oatmeal reaches the desired consistency. Stir in the coconut oil.

3 Remove the saucepan from the heat, and stir any of the desired additions into the oatmeal. Cover and let stand for 5 minutes.

4 Divide the oatmeal between 2 bowls, top each with flaxseeds, and serve. If desired, pour on some almond milk or drizzle on some honey.

FOR A CHANGE

◆ If you have to avoid gluten, make sure that the oatmeal you buy is marked "gluten-free." Because of cross-contamination at the farm and in production facilities, most of the oatmeal you'll find on store shelves contains some gluten. To be safe, check the package label.

Super Salads

Salads are a bridge that takes you from a cooked foods lifestyle to a living foods lifestyle. The super salads on the following pages are fun to prepare, highly versatile, and always satisfying. Don't forget, though, that these aren't the only salads offered in our book. For more salad ideas, turn to our "Basic Recipes" section, which begins on page 85. And if you want to create your own living salads using your favorite ingredients, turn to the inset on page 98.

Jay's Favorite Salad

Jay loves to pair this salad with a hearty veggie juice drink. Try a glass of Power-Up Digestive (see page 168).

5 cups (375 g) baby field greens

1 cup (75 g) baby spinach

1 cup (150 g) grated carrots

1 cup (150 g) grated yellow summer squash or zucchini

1 large vine-ripened tomato, chopped

$1/2$ cup (50 g) chopped scallions (green onions)

$1/2$ cup (63 g) chopped walnuts

$1/2$ cup (75 g) raisins

$1/3$ cup (21 g) pumpkin seeds

1 recipe Superfast Tahini Dressing (see page 117)

SERVINGS: 4   80% LIVING

1 Place the field greens and spinach in a large bowl, and toss to mix. Then toss in the remaining salad ingredients.

2 Directly before serving, add the desired amount of the prepared dressing to the salad, and toss until the ingredients are well coated. Serve.

FOR A CHANGE

◆ For a more substantial meal, heat 4 spinach tortillas (gluten-free, if necessary) and use the salad as a filling. You'll want to use a generous amount of dressing so that the tortillas are well-moistened by the salad.

Creating Your Own Super Green Salads

Salads are the core of our living foods eating program. We highly recommend eating at least one large salad per day—for lunch, for dinner, or for both meals. When you start making these dishes part of your daily menu, you will find that your energy multiplies and your digestion becomes smoother and easier. Over the years, I've learned that salads are most satisfying when they combine several different tastes and textures. Some tastes you may want to combine in as many salads as possible include sweet (like raisins), bitter/astringent (like herbs), and salty (like capers). Also be sure to include contrasting textures, like crisp (romaine), chewy (like rice), and crunchy (like slivered almonds). You and your family will appreciate the vari-ety, and your body will appreciate the galaxy of nutrients that these ingredients provide.

This section presents recipes for a range of different salads, including super green salads like Seaweed Spinach Salad. But once you embark on your living foods lifestyle, you'll almost certainly want to create your own living green salads to suit your tastes. For the best nutrition and satisfaction, I suggest following our creative green salad pyramid, shown below. Build a base of greens, and then add veggies, sprouts, herbs, nuts, grains, and fresh or dried fruits. The lists found after the pyramid include healthy ingredient choices. Pick your favorites, and you'll be sure to create delicious, nutritious super salads that your family will love.

Fresh and Dried Fruits

Grains and Beans

Nuts and Seeds

Herbs and Other Bitter or Salty Foods

Sprouts

Vegetables

Salad Greens

Salad Greens

Arugula

Butter lettuce

Cabbage (red, green, or napa), shredded

Endive

Escarole

Field greens (regular or baby)

Kale

Red leaf lettuce

Romaine lettuce

Spinach (regular or baby)

Swiss chard

Vegetables

Asparagus, steamed and sliced

Beets, julienned

Bell peppers (green, orange, red, or yellow), julienned

Broccoli, small florets

Brussels sprouts, very thinly sliced

Carrots, julienned

Cauliflower, small florets

Celery, chopped or diced

Corn kernels

Cucumbers, chopped

Edamame (fresh soybeans), cooked

Fennel, thinly sliced

Green beans, steamed and/or cut in 1-inch pieces

Jerusalem artichokes, thinly sliced

Jicama, julienned

Peas

Potatoes (red, white, or yellow), steamed and sliced

Summer squash, sliced or chopped

Tomatoes (any kind), chopped

Turnips, julienned

Zucchini, julienned

Sprouts

Adzuki bean

Alfalfa

Bean

Broccoli

Fenugreek

Lentil

Mung bean

Sunflower

Herbs and Other Bitter or Salty Additions

Basil

Capers

Chives

Cilantro

Dill

Garlic

Leeks, sliced thinly

Mint leaves

Olives

Onions (any type), chopped or sliced

Parsley

Radicchio

Radish

Scallions (green onions), sliced or chopped

Shallots, chopped

Tarragon

Nuts and Seeds

Almonds, slivered

Cashews, chopped

Filberts, chopped

Hemp seeds

Macadamia nuts, chopped

Peanuts, whole or chopped

Pecans, chopped

Pumpkin seeds (regular or tamari)

Sunflower seeds

Walnuts, chopped

Grains, Beans, and Other Chewy Additions

Adzuki beans

Barley (pearl)

Black beans

Black-eyed peas

Brown rice (long or short grain)

Bulgur wheat

Couscous

Garbanzo beans

Lentils (brown or green)

Millet

Mung beans

Navy beans

Quinoa

Tofu or sprouted tofu (firm, extra-firm, or medium-firm), cubed or crumbled

Wild rice

Fruits

Apples (fresh), grated or diced

Apricots (fresh or dried), chopped

Avocados (preferably Haas), diced

Blueberries

Coconuts (fresh or dried), chopped or grated

Cranberries (dried)

Currants (fresh or dried)

Dates (fresh or dried), chopped

Figs (fresh or dried), chopped

Pears, sliced or chopped

Raisins

Strawberries, sliced

Seaweed Spinach Salad

This is a wonderful salad, especially for women, since research shows that the nutrients in seaweed support female hormones.

3 cups (225 g) baby field greens

1/2 cup (38 g) baby spinach

1/2 cup (75 g) julienned or grated carrots

1/2 cup (88 g) julienned or grated zucchini

1/2 cup (88 g) julienned or grated red bell pepper

1/2 cup (72 g) sunflower seeds

1/2 cup (32 g) pumpkin seeds

3 sheets toasted nori, broken into 1-inch pieces

Dressing

1/2 cup (118 ml) extra virgin olive oil

1 tablespoon tamari or Bragg Liquid Aminos

1 teaspoon sesame oil

2 cloves garlic

1 teaspoon chopped fresh tarragon

Pinch cayenne pepper

SERVINGS: 4   100% LIVING

1 To make the dressing, place all of the dressing ingredients in a blender and process until smooth. Set aside.

2 To make the salad, place all of the salad ingredients in a large bowl, and toss to mix.

3 Directly before serving, add the desired amount of the prepared dressing to the salad, and toss until the ingredients are well coated. Serve.

FOR A CHANGE

◆ If you have to avoid gluten, be sure to buy a gluten-free brand of tamari or to use Bragg Liquid Aminos, which is gluten-free.

◆ For a heartier dish, toss a cup of cooked brown rice into the salad.

Healthy Protein Salad

Loaded with protein, this salad is a complete meal—and it's completely delicious, as well. Pair it with Meal Sipper Digestive, found on page 167.

2 cups (150 g) bite-sized pieces romaine lettuce

2 cups (150 g) baby spinach

$^1/_2$ cup (75 g) cashews

1 cup (100 g) lentil sprouts or your favorite sprouts (see page 102 for sprouting instructions)

$^1/_2$ cup (50 g) bean sprouts (see page 102 for sprouting instructions)

1 carrot, grated or julienned

$^1/_2$ cup (32 g) pumpkin seeds

$^1/_2$ cup (13 g) minced fresh parsley

2 small avocados (preferably Haas), peeled and chopped

1 large vine-ripened tomato, chopped

1 small scallion (green onion), chopped (for garnish)

1 recipe Sun-Dried Tomato Tahini Dressing (see page 122) or Fresh Herb Salad Dressing (see page 118)

SERVINGS: 4   100% LIVING

1 Place all of the salad ingredients except for the avocado, tomato, and scallion in a large bowl. Toss to mix.

2 Directly before serving, add the desired amount of the prepared dressing to the salad, and toss until the ingredients are well coated. Distribute the chopped avocado and tomato over the top of the salad, and garnish with a sprinkling of scallions. Serve.

Sprouting Basics

Sprouting dried beans, grains, or seeds from various edible plants takes relatively little effort and offers a number of benefits. When sprouted, these foods become easier to digest and require little or no cooking. Best of all, their nutritional content, especially vitamin C, increases significantly.

Just about any whole unbroken raw seed, grain, or dried bean can be sprouted. Popular choices include sunflower, chia, mung, mustard, radish, and alfalfa seeds; grains like barley, buckwheat, millet, oats, and wheat berries; and beans and legumes such as adzuki beans, garbanzos, and lentils. Seeds for sprouting are available in most natural foods stores. Be sure to choose those that are organic and specifically cultivated for sprouting, not for growing in your garden. Seeds sold for gardening are sometimes treated with chemicals.

Depending on the size of the seeds being sprouted, we use one of the following very simple methods—the bowl-and-strainer method or the jar method. It's important to remove any broken seeds or beans before using either method.

Bowl-and-Strainer Method

This is the preferred method for sprouting beans and larger seeds, such as wheat berries, garbanzo beans, mung beans, adzuki beans, and sunflower seeds.

1. Rinse the seeds/beans, then place them in a bowl that is large enough for them to more than double in size without being crowded. Add enough fresh cool (not cold) water to generously cover. Let soak about eight hours or overnight.

2. Drain the soaked seeds/beans through a strainer, rinse under fresh running water, and drain well.

3. Return the seeds/beans to the bowl and leave on the counter (out of the sunlight). Continue rinsing and draining two or three times a day for one to three days. The sprouts are ready when they are $1/4$ to $1/2$ inch long.

1. Soak the seeds in cool water.

2. Drain the seeds before returning them to the bowl.

Jar Method

For sprouting smaller seeds, like alfalfa, mustard, and radish, this method is recommended. You will need a large wide-mouth jar—a quart-size mason jar is good—and either a piece of cheesecloth or a nylon stocking that is large enough to stretch across the opening. Special sprouting jars with screen tops are also available. For this size jar, we generally sprout one or two tablespoons of seeds.

1. Rinse the seeds, place them in the jar, and add enough fresh cool (not cold) water to generously cover. Cover the opening of the jar with a piece of cheesecloth or nylon stocking and secure it tightly with a rubber band. Let the seeds soak about eight hours or overnight.

2. Drain the soaked seeds through the fabric top. The fabric will catch the seeds and keep them in the jar.

3. Add fresh water (right through the fabric top) and rinse the seeds gently but thoroughly. Drain the water from the jar. It is important to drain the seeds well. They should not be sitting in water at this point.

4. Leave the jar on the counter (out of sunlight), and continue rinsing and draining the seeds two or three times a day for four to five days. When the sprouts fill the jar, place them on a sunny windowsill, and within twenty-four hours, they will turn green. Now they are ready to eat or juice.

1. Soak the seeds in cool water.

2. Drain the seeds.

3. Allow the drained seeds to sprout.

Mid-Eastern Salad

High-protein quinoa makes this salad satisfying, and the combination of vegetables, fruits, and herbs gives it Mid-Eastern flair. If possible, prepare this dish the day before you serve it to allow the flavors to blend. Then serve it over a bed of leafy greens for a complete meal. Power-Up Digestive on page 168 makes a great accompanying beverage.

3 cups (585 g) cooked quinoa

2 cucumbers, peeled and chopped

2 or 3 vine-ripened tomatoes, seeded and chopped

2 $^{1}/_{2}$ cups (63 g) chopped fresh mint

1 $^{1}/_{2}$ cups (225 g) dark raisins

$^{1}/_{2}$ cup (70 g) chopped olives of your choice

$^{1}/_{2}$ cup (50 g) chopped scallions (green onions)

$^{1}/_{2}$ cup (13 g) minced fresh parsley

$^{3}/_{4}$ cup (177 ml) fresh lemon juice

$^{1}/_{3}$ cup (79 ml) extra virgin olive oil

3 cloves garlic, minced

Sea salt and cayenne pepper to taste

SERVINGS: 4   75% LIVING

1 Place the quinoa, cucumbers, tomatoes, mint, raisins, olives, scallions, and parsley in a large bowl, and toss to mix well.

2 Stir the lemon juice, olive oil, and garlic into the quinoa mixture, tossing to coat. Season to taste with salt and cayenne pepper.

3 Cover the salad and chill for at least several hours before serving.

FOR A CHANGE

◆ Serve this over our Basic Salad (see page 85) for a complete meal.

◆ Add some of the salad to the filling of the Tofu Tacos (see page 150).

◆ Wrap the filling inside large green cabbage leaves. (This is Linda's favorite. Try it!)

Mock Tuna Salad

This salad is delicious as a sandwich filling, served atop a green salad, or accompanied by flax seed crackers. Pair this dish with a glass of Heavy-Duty Green Digestive (see page 166).

2 cups (488 g) cooked
    garbanzo beans

$^1/_2$ cup (50 g) diced celery

$^1/_2$ cup (123 g) pickle relish

$^1/_2$ cup (118 ml) sesame oil

$^1/_3$ cup (45 g) nutritional yeast

2 teaspoons tamari or Bragg
    Liquid Aminos

1 teaspoon kelp powder

$^1/_2$ teaspoon sea salt

$^1/_8$ teaspoon black pepper

$^1/_8$ teaspoon cayenne pepper

SERVINGS: 4   20% LIVING

1 Place all of the ingredients in a blender or food processor, and pulse until the desired consistency is reached.

2 Serve immediately or chill until serving.

FOR A CHANGE

◆ If you have to avoid gluten, be sure to buy a gluten-free brand of tamari or to use Bragg Liquid Aminos, which is gluten-free.

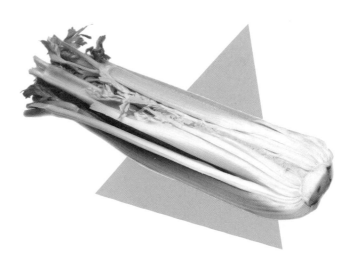

Better Than Egg Salad

Like our Mock Tuna Salad (see page 105), Better Than Egg Salad is wonderful over greens or as a sandwich filling. It's also delicious with flax seed crackers, either homemade or store-bought. Pair it with Green Power Tummy Remedy (see page 166) and enjoy!

1 pound (454 g) extra-firm tofu*

2 large celery stalks, diced

$^1/_2$ cup (70 g) chopped black olives

$^1/_2$ cup (75 mg) diced yellow onion

$^1/_3$ cup (80 g) Nayonnaise or any egg-free mayonnaise

1 tablespoon Dijon mustard

1 clove garlic, minced

Pinch cayenne pepper

Sea salt and black pepper to taste

*An especially healthy choice is non-GMO organic sprouted tofu.

SERVINGS: 2–4   20% LIVING

1 To squeeze the excess water out of the tofu, place the block of tofu between two paper towels and use your hands to press out the liquid. Get the tofu as dry as possible to prevent the salad from becoming watery.

2 Crumble the dried tofu into a large bowl. Add the celery, olives, and onion, and toss to mix. Stir in the Nayonnaise, mustard, and garlic, and season to taste with salt and pepper.

3 Serve immediately or chill until serving.

New York Cabbage Salad

This beautiful salad incorporates a rainbow of colors and a variety of flavors. Just as important, it's a 100-percent living meal. A glass of Three "C's" Digestive Juice (see page 169) is the perfect complement.

1 head romaine lettuce, diced

1 $^1/_2$ cups (150 g) diced red and green cabbage

1 medium-sized apple, diced

$^1/_2$ cup (43 g) sliced almonds

$^1/_2$ cup (75 g) raisins

$^1/_2$ cup (13 g) chopped fresh cilantro

$^1/_3$ cup (58 g) pomegranate seeds or dried cranberries

Dressing

$^1/_2$ cup (118 ml) macadamia nut oil

$^1/_3$ cup (79 ml) apple cider vinegar

2 tablespoons fresh lime juice

1 tablespoon honey or 2 tablespoons coconut sugar

Sea salt and cayenne pepper to taste

SERVINGS: 4   100% LIVING

1 To make the dressing, place all of the dressing ingredients in a small bowl, and whisk until well-blended. Set aside.

2 To make the salad, place all of the salad ingredients in a large bowl, and toss to mix.

3 Directly before serving, add the desired amount of the prepared dressing to the salad and toss until the ingredients are well coated. Serve.

Super Salad with Black Beans

Our kids loved this salad when they were little! Serve it as is, use it as a filling for wraps, or add a scoop of Homemade Hummus (see page 208) before serving.

2 cups (150 g) shredded romaine lettuce

2 cups (66 g) alfalfa sprouts (see page 102 for sprouting instructions)

1 1/2 cups (351 g) cooked black beans

1 cup (77 g) lentil sprouts or your favorite sprouts (see page 102 for sprouting instructions)

1 cup (150 g) julienned carrots

6 scallions (green onions), chopped

3 avocados (preferably Haas), peeled and diced

2 medium-sized tomatoes, chopped

1 medium-sized cucumber, peeled and sliced

1 recipe Superfast Tahini Dressing (see page 117)

SERVINGS: 2   80% LIVING

1 Place all of the salad ingredients in a large bowl, and toss to mix well.

2 Directly before serving, add the desired amount of the prepared dressing to the salad, and toss until the ingredients are well coated. Serve.

FOR A CHANGE

◆ This makes a great filling for wraps! Heat 4 spinach tortillas (gluten-free, if necessary) to make them pliable, spoon on some of the filling, and fold it into a neat package. Another option is to layer the separate ingredients over the tortillas one at a time. Start with the beans and follow with the avocado, carrot, tomatoes, cucumber, lettuce, sprouts, scallions, and salsa. If you like your tortillas moister, add a little more dressing to the wrap.

"To wish to be well is a part of becoming well."
—Seneca, Philosopher

Asian Salad

This hearty rice-based salad offers a surprising mix of flavors with a tantalizing Asian twist. Serve it with a glass of Green Power Tummy Remedy (see page 166).

4 cups (1 kg) hot cooked brown rice

6 scallions (green onions), minced

$1/2$ cup (75 g) chopped cashews

$1/2$ cup (88g) chopped dates

$1/2$ cup (13 g) minced fresh parsley

$1/2$ cup (13 g) minced fresh cilantro

2 tablespoons chopped fresh mint

1 tablespoon chopped fresh dill

1 tomato, chopped (for garnish)

Dressing

$1/4$ cup (59 ml) olive oil

3 tablespoons tamari or Bragg Liquid Aminos

$1/4$ teaspoon black pepper

SERVINGS: 4–6   60–75% LIVING

1 To make the dressing, place all of the dressing ingredients in a small bowl, and whisk until well blended. Set aside.

2 To make the salad, place the hot rice in a large mixing bowl. Add all of the remaining salad ingredients except for the tomato, and toss to mix.

3 Add the desired amount of the prepared dressing to the salad, and toss until the ingredients are well coated. Scatter the chopped tomato over the top, and serve.

FOR A CHANGE

◆ If you have to avoid gluten, be sure to buy a gluten-free brand of tamari or to use Bragg Liquid Aminos, which is gluten-free.

◆ For a change of pace, toss a diced avocado into the salad or top the salad with sliced avocado.

Simple Walnut Rice Salad

Enjoy this simple yet delicious dish as is or—to increase the living foods in your meal—combine it with our Basic Salad (see page 85). For the perfect accompanying beverage, try Salad Tonic Digestive (see page 169).

2 cups (500 g) cooked brown rice

1 cup (150 g) grated carrots

1 cup (125 g) chopped walnuts

1 cup (175 g) shredded zucchini

1 cup (about 80 g) sprouts of your choice, such as lentil or alfalfa (see page 102 for sprouting instructions)

1 scallion (green onion), chopped

Dressing

3 tablespoons Bragg Liquid Aminos

2 tablespoons sesame oil

1 tablespoon fresh lemon juice

4 large leaves basil

2 cloves garlic

SERVINGS: 4   60–75% LIVING

1 To make the dressing, place all of the ingredients in a blender, and process until smooth. Set aside.

2 To make the salad, place all of the salad ingredients in a large bowl, and toss to mix.

3 Add the desired amount of the prepared dressing to the salad, and toss until the ingredients are well coated. Serve.

Millet Basil Salad

Packed with nutrition, our Millet Basil Salad is also very versatile, as the flavor and texture can be changed by swapping out the millet for another grain. Accompany the dish with Popeye's Digestive Special (see page 168).

3 cups (522 g) cooked millet

1 cup (75g) chopped romaine lettuce

1 cup (75 g) baby spinach

1 cup (150 g) julienned carrot

$^1/_2$ cup (75 g) diced cucumber

$^1/_3$ cup (15 g) chopped basil

$^1/_4$ cup (38 g) diced white onion

$^1/_2$ cup (100 g) chopped tomato

$^1/_2$ cup (13 g) chopped fresh cilantro or parsley

2 tablespoons diced scallions (green onions)

1 recipe Macadamia Oil Dressing (see page 121)

SERVINGS: 2–4   70–80% LIVING

1 Place the millet, lettuce, spinach, carrot, cucumber, basil, and onion in a large bowl, and toss to mix.

2 Add the desired amount of the prepared dressing to the salad, and toss until the ingredients are well coated.

3 Distribute the tomato, cilantro or parsley, and scallions over the top of the salad, and serve.

FOR A CHANGE

◆ Give this salad a new spin by replacing the millet with your favorite cooked grain, such as brown rice, quinoa, or bulgur wheat. If you are following a gluten-free diet, avoid the bulgur wheat because it contains gluten.

◆ Toss in $^1/_2$ cup of pumpkin seeds to add a nutty taste and a little crunch.

◆ Subtly change the flavor of the dressing by replacing the macadamia nut oil with avocado oil, walnut oil, hemp oil, or flaxseed oil.

South of the Border Salad

Fresh cilantro, avocado, onion, and a lemony dressing lend this salad lively South of the Border flavor. For a perfect meal, pair it with Heavy-Duty Green Digestive (see page 166).

1 cup (75 g) chopped red leaf lettuce

1 cup (75 g) chopped romaine lettuce

1 cup (244 g) cooked garbanzo beans or your favorite beans

4 medium-sized tomatoes, chopped

2 avocados (preferably Haas), peeled and diced

$^{1}/_{2}$ cup (13 g) chopped fresh cilantro

$^{1}/_{4}$ yellow onion, diced

1 recipe Super Green Salad Dressing (see page 120)

SERVINGS: 2   **75–80% LIVING**

1 Place all of the salad ingredients in a large bowl, and toss to mix.

2 Directly before serving, add the desired amount of the prepared dressing to the salad, and toss until the ingredients are well coated. Serve.

FOR A CHANGE:

◆ For a fun pick-up meal, wrap portions of the salad in large lettuce leaves or spinach tortillas (gluten-free, if desired).

Jay's Beet-Apple Salad

Jay loves this salad in the fall, when the apples are especially crisp and juicy. As a plus, the combination of apples and raw beet enhances liver and gallbladder function. To further promote liver health, serve with a glass of the Liver Mover (see page 181).

4 cups (300 g) chopped red leaf or romaine lettuce

2 Golden Delicious or Granny Smith apples, diced

1 medium-sized beet, peeled and julienned

$^1/_2$ cup (63 g) chopped walnuts

Dressing

3 tablespoons fresh lemon juice

1 teaspoon mustard

1 clove garlic

$^1/_3$ cup (79 ml) walnut oil

Sea salt and cayenne or black pepper to taste

SERVINGS: 2   100% LIVING

1 To make the dressing, place the lemon juice, mustard, and garlic in a blender. Slowly add the oil in a stream while the blender is processing. Season to taste with salt and pepper, and set aside.

2 To make the salad, place all of the salad ingredients in a large bowl, and toss to mix.

3 Directly before serving, add the desired amount of the prepared dressing to the salad, and toss until the ingredients are well coated. Serve.

FOR A CHANGE

◆ Add slices of in-season ripe pear to the finished salad, tossing the pear with the other ingredients or arranging it over the top of the dish just before serving.

Super Salad Dressings

In the following pages, you'll find a special collection of dressings designed to enliven salads, add a splash of flavor to living soups, and moisten and enhance tostadas, tacos, and wraps. Rich and savory, these dressings can make even the simplest salad or wrap deeply satisfying, which is so important when you're switching to a living foods diet.

When following these taste-testing recipes, please choose the highest-quality oils. By using the oils we recommend and selecting only products that are organic, unrefined, and extracted mechanically rather than with chemicals or heat, you will not only make your dressings more delicious but will also enhance your heart-health and avoid unwholesome additives.

Tofu Tarragon Tomato Dressing

Featuring the tang of tomatoes and the creaminess of tofu, this tarragon-flavored dressing is delicious on green salads and grain salads alike.

1 medium-sized vine-ripened
  tomato, cut into chunks

1/4 cup (59 ml) apple cider vinegar

3 tablespoons silken tofu

2 tablespoons chopped
  fresh tarragon

2 cloves garlic

1 teaspoon mustard

1 teaspoon black pepper

1/2 teaspoon sea salt

Pinch cayenne pepper

1/2 cup extra virgin olive oil

YIELD: 2/3 CUP   100% LIVING

1 Place all of the ingredients except for the olive oil in a blender, and blend until smooth.

2 Slowly add the oil in a stream while the blender is processing. Blend until the mixture has thickened.

3 Use immediately, or place in an airtight container and refrigerate for up to three days.

Heart-Smart Omega-3 Dressing

Omega-3-rich flax oil makes this dressing heart-healthy, and fresh herbs make it delicious.

$^1/_2$ cup (118 ml) extra virgin olive oil

$^1/_3$ cup (79 ml) flax oil

$^1/_4$ cup (59 ml) rice vinegar or apple cider vinegar

1 tablespoon honey or agave nectar

1 tablespoon minced fresh basil

1 tablespoon minced fresh tarragon

1 tablespoon minced fresh oregano

4 cloves garlic

1 $^1/_2$ teaspoons Spike seasoning blend

Pinch black pepper

YIELD: 1 CUP   100% LIVING

1 Place all of the ingredients in a blender, and blend until smooth.

2 Use immediately, or place in an airtight container and refrigerate for up to three days.

FOR A CHANGE

◆ For more heat, replace the Spike seasoning with a Cajun seasoning blend.

◆ For a different flavor, replace the basil and tarragon with parsley or cilantro.

Royal Thai Salad Dressing

Use this dressing to give an exotic spin to any salad, or substitute it for the dressing in our luscious Asian Salad (see page 109).

1 cup (237 ml) fresh
 orange juice

1/4 cup (59 ml) rice vinegar

1 teaspoon minced
 fresh ginger

1 teaspoon chopped garlic

1 tablespoon tamari or Bragg
 Liquid Aminos

2 tablespoons toasted
 sesame oil

Pinch cayenne pepper

YIELD: 1 1/3 CUPS   100% LIVING

1 Place all of the ingredients in a blender, and blend until smooth.

2 Use immediately, or place in an airtight container and refrigerate for up to three days.

FOR A CHANGE

◆ If you have to avoid gluten, be sure to buy a gluten-free brand of tamari or to use Bragg Liquid Aminos, which is gluten-free.

Superfast Tahini Dressing

The perfect salad dressing when you're pressed for time, this is a favorite in our family. It also makes a tasty addition to living soups.

1/4 cup (59 ml) tahini

1/4 cup (59 ml) fresh
 lemon juice

2 tablespoons brown miso

1 small clove garlic

Pinch cayenne pepper

Pinch sea salt

YIELD: 1/2 CUP   100% LIVING

1 Place all of the ingredients in a blender, and blend until smooth.

2 Use immediately, or place in an airtight container and refrigerate for up to five days.

FOR A CHANGE

◆ If you have to avoid gluten, make sure that the miso you use is marked "gluten-free."

Fresh Herb Salad Dressing

This light green dressing adds wonderful color and flavor to Vegetarian Tacos (see page 149). It can also be poured over any living soup for a burst of fresh herb taste and a delightfully smooth consistency. It is one of our favorite dressings.

³/₄ cup (19 g) chopped fresh dill

¹/₂ cup (38 g) baby spinach

¹/₂ cup (13 g) chopped fresh parsley

¹/₂ cup (13 g) chopped fresh cilantro

¹/₃ cup (50 g) chopped yellow onion

2 cloves garlic

¹/₂ cup (118 ml) water

2 tablespoons balsamic vinegar or apple cider vinegar

1 tablespoon tamari or Bragg Liquid Aminos

Pinch cayenne pepper

1 cup (237 ml) extra virgin olive oil or grape seed oil

YIELD: ³/₄ CUP   100% LIVING

1 Place all of the ingredients except for the olive oil in a blender, and blend until smooth.

2 Slowly add the oil in a stream while the blender is processing. Blend until the mixture has thickened.

3 Use immediately, or place in an airtight container and refrigerate for up to three days.

FOR A CHANGE

◆ If you have to avoid gluten, be sure to buy a gluten-free brand of tamari or to use Bragg Liquid Aminos, which is gluten-free.

Superfast Tofu Dressing

A snap to prepare, this dressing can be tossed with a salad that includes nuts or seeds, poured over steamed veggies and rice, or used as a creamy dip for raw vegetables. It was always one of our kids' favorites!

8 ounces (224 g) silken or soft tofu

2 tablespoons fresh lemon juice

2 tablespoons extra virgin olive oil

1 tablespoon chopped fresh parsley or cilantro

1 clove garlic

$1/_2$ teaspoon sea salt

$1/_8$ teaspoon black pepper

YIELD: 1$^1/_4$ CUPS   60% LIVING

1 Place all of the ingredients in a blender, and blend until smooth.

2 Use immediately, or place in an airtight container and refrigerate for up to three days.

No-Fat Herb Dressing

Whether you're watching your weight or, instead of putting your healthy fats in your dressing, you prefer to put them in your salad—perhaps in the form of a creamy avocado— this flavorful mixture will fit the bill.

$3/_4$ cup (177 ml) fresh tomato juice

$1/_4$ cup (59 ml) apple cider vinegar

$1/_4$ teaspoon honey or liquid stevia

1 tablespoon chopped fresh parsley

1 tablespoon chopped chives or scallions (green onions)

1 clove garlic

$1/_2$ teaspoon sea salt

Pinch each dried oregano, black pepper, and cayenne pepper

YIELD: 1 CUP   100% LIVING

1 Place all of the ingredients in a blender, and blend until smooth.

2 Use immediately, or place in an airtight container and refrigerate for up to three days.

Super Green Salad Dressing

Bursting with the tastes of summer, this dressing is also rich in antioxidants.

$^{1}/_{4}$ cup (25 g) chopped scallions
(green onions)

$^{1}/_{4}$ cup (6 g) chopped fresh parsley

$^{1}/_{4}$ cup (6 g) chopped fresh cilantro

$^{1}/_{4}$ cup (19 g) baby spinach

$^{1}/_{4}$ cup (59 ml) apple cider vinegar

2 tablespoons fresh lemon juice

2 cloves garlic, pressed

1 teaspoon chopped fresh tarragon

1 teaspoon sea salt

Black pepper and cayenne pepper
to taste

$^{1}/_{2}$ cup (118 ml) extra virgin
olive oil

YIELD: 1 CUP   100% LIVING

1 Place all of the ingredients except for the olive oil in a blender, and blend until smooth.

2 Slowly add the oil in a stream while the blender is processing. Blend until the mixture has thickened.

3 Use immediately, or place in an airtight container and refrigerate for up to three days.

Macadamia Oil Dressing

This healthy and delicious dressing gets its rich, buttery flavor from macadamia nut oil. Toss it into a summer salad, drizzle it over a living soup, or use it as a tasty addition to Tofu Tacos (see page 150).

$^1/_4$ cup (6 g) chopped fresh parsley

$^1/_4$ cup (6 g) chopped fresh cilantro

$^1/_4$ cup (19 g) baby spinach

$^1/_4$ cup (59 ml) apple cider vinegar

2 tablespoons fresh lemon juice

1 teaspoon Dijon mustard

1 teaspoon sea salt

Black pepper and cayenne pepper to taste

$^1/_2$ cup (118 ml) macadamia nut oil

YIELD: 1 CUP   100% LIVING

1 Place all of the ingredients except for the macadamia nut oil in a blender, and blend until smooth.

2 Slowly add the oil in a stream while the blender is processing. Blend until the mixture has thickened.

3 Use immediately, or place in an airtight container and refrigerate for up to three days.

FOR A CHANGE

◆ This dressing is wonderfully versatile. For a different flavor, replace the macadamia nut oil with avocado oil, walnut oil, hemp oil, or flaxseed oil.

Sun-Dried Tomato Tahini Dressing

The night before you plan to serve this dressing, place the sun-dried tomatoes in the olive oil, cover, and allow the mixture to sit overnight. The next day, you'll be able complete the recipe in no time flat.

8 sun-dried tomatoes (packed without oil)

1/4 cup plus 2 tablespoons (90 ml) extra virgin olive oil

2 tablespoons tahini

2 teaspoons fresh lemon or lime juice

1 1/2 teaspoons white or brown miso

1 clove garlic

1 teaspoon sea salt

1/2 teaspoon crushed red pepper

1/2 cup (118 ml) water

YIELD: 3/4 CUP   100% LIVING

1 Place the sun-dried tomatoes in a small bowl, and add the olive oil. Cover and allow to sit overnight.

2 The next day, place the reserved sun-dried tomatoes and oil in a blender along with all of the remaining ingredients except for the water. Process for one or two minutes, or until the ingredients are liquefied.

3 Slowly add the water in a stream while the blender is processing. Use only enough water to achieve the desired consistency.

4 Use immediately, or place in an airtight container and refrigerate for up to three days.

FOR A CHANGE

◆ If you have to avoid gluten, make sure that the miso you use is marked "gluten-free."

◆ If you want to use this dressing as a topping for veggie burgers or sandwiches, or as a sauce for Nutty Rice and Veggies (see page 141), decrease the amount of water listed in the recipe so that the mixture is nice and thick.

Carrot Juice Veggie Dressing

Bursting with nutrients, this dressing beautifully complements salads that contain nuts and seeds, as well as mixtures of shredded vegetables.

4 large carrots

Handful parsley

Handful cilantro

1 medium-sized tomato, cut into pieces

$^1/_2$ red bell pepper, cut into pieces

$^1/_2$ teaspoon minced jalapeño pepper

$^1/_2$ teaspoon chopped fresh tarragon

1 clove garlic

2 tablespoons red miso

2 tablespoons tahini

2 tablespoons fresh lemon or lime juice

Sea salt and black pepper to taste

$^1/_3$ cup (79 ml) extra virgin olive oil

YIELD: 1 $^1/_2$ CUPS   100% LIVING

1 Juice the carrots, parsley, and cilantro together so that the carrot juice prevents the greens from getting stuck inside the juicer. This will yield about 1 cup of juice. Reserve all but $^3/_4$ cup for another use.

2 Place $^3/_4$ cup of the carrot-herb juice in a blender along with all of the remaining ingredients except for the olive oil. Process until the ingredients are completely liquefied.

3 Slowly add the olive in a stream while the blender is processing.

4 Use immediately, or place in an airtight container and refrigerate for up to two days.

FOR A CHANGE

◆ If you have to avoid gluten, make sure that the miso you use is marked "gluten-free."

"About eighty percent of the food on shelves of supermarkets today didn't exist 100 years ago."

—Larry McCleary, Physician

Living Breakfasts

Living breakfasts are the only way to go! The choices on the following pages are delicious, satisfying, visually beautiful, and easy to prepare. Be aware, though, that plenty of other living breakfast ideas are provided throughout this book. For instance, both Carrot and Coconut Juice (see page 162) and Date a Banana for Breakfast Smoothie (see page 192) can serve as complete early-morning meals. As you continue to learn about living foods and page through the recipes in Part Three, you'll find other options that are not only delectable, but also provide the energy you need to start your day.

Cinnamon, Spice 'n Everything Nice Granola

This granola serves as both a delicious breakfast and an enjoyable anytime snack!

5 cups (500 g) uncooked rolled oats

1 cup (125 g) chopped walnuts

1 cup (112 g) chopped almonds

1 cup (150 g) raisins

$1/2$ cup (72 g) sunflower seeds

$1/2$ cup (32 g) pumpkin seeds

$1/2$ cup (38 g) shredded unsweetened coconut

$1/2$ cup (90 g) flax seeds

$1/2$ cup (58 g) sesame seeds

$1/2$ teaspoon ground cinnamon

$1/2$ teaspoon ground nutmeg

$1/2$ teaspoon ground anise

SERVINGS: 10   100% LIVING

1 Place all of the ingredients in a large bowl and mix together well.

2 Divide the cereal among individual bowls, topping with your favorite fresh nut milk, if desired. Let sit 5 to 10 minutes and allow the milk to soften the oats before eating.

3 Place leftovers in an airtight container and store in the pantry for up to two months.

FOR A CHANGE

◆ If you have to avoid gluten, make sure that the oatmeal you buy is marked "gluten-free." Because of cross-contamination at the farm and in production facilities, most of the oatmeal you'll find on store shelves contains some gluten. To be safe, check the package label.

Breakfast Pie

We usually prepare this fresh fruit pie the night before, so we can enjoy it for breakfast in the morning.

Strawberry Cream Topping

1 pound (450 g) strawberries

1 baby coconut and its liquid*

$^1/_2$ cup (75 g) macadamia nuts

1 tablespoon honey, or 2 tablespoons coconut sugar

1 teaspoon ground nutmeg

$^1/_2$ teaspoon ground cinnamon

Crust

$1^1/_2$ cups (210 g) sunflower seeds

$^1/_2$ cup (112 g) pitted dates

Filling

2 bananas, sliced

3 kiwis, peeled and sliced

15 strawberries, thinly sliced

* See page 91 for preparation instructions.

SERVINGS: 6   100% LIVING

1 Place all of the strawberry cream ingredients in a blender, and blend until thick and creamy. Refrigerate for 1 hour.

2 To prepare the crust, place the sunflower seeds and dates in a food processor, and blend for about 1 minute, or until the mixture begins to clump. (It will be a bit warm.)

3 Transfer the mixture to an 11-inch pie pan (preferably glass) and press it evenly on the bottom and sides to form a crust. Refrigerate for about 10 minutes to cool.

4 Arrange a layer of banana slices on top of the cooled crust, followed by a layer of sliced kiwis, and another layer of sliced strawberries. Repeat the layers.

5 Spoon the prepared strawberry cream on top and refrigerate for at least 1 hour before serving. Store leftovers in the refrigerator for up to two days.

Apricot and Almond Delight

This delicious breakfast cereal is rich in protein and complex carbohydrates. It's also one of our wintertime favorites. Enjoy it topped with freshly chopped apples or pears, or a handful of crushed cranberries.

$^{1}/_{2}$ cup (56 g) slivered almonds

$^{2}/_{3}$ cup (100g) dried apricots, soaked for 1 hour and drained

2 cups (200 g) uncooked rolled oats, soaked for 30 minutes and drained

$^{1}/_{3}$ cup (120 g) flax seeds

$^{1}/_{2}$ cup (50 g) hemp seeds

$^{1}/_{2}$ cup (75 g) raisins

SERVINGS: 4   100% LIVING

1 Place all of the ingredients in a large mixing bowl, and stir well to combine.

2 Divide the cereal among individual bowls, topping with fresh Living Almond Milk (see page 186), if desired.

FOR A CHANGE

◆ If you have to avoid gluten, make sure that the oatmeal you buy is marked "gluten-free." Because of cross-contamination at the farm and in production facilities, most of the oatmeal you'll find on store shelves contains some gluten. To be safe, check the package label.

◆ For added flavor, serve this cereal with a drizzle of honey or a sprinkling of ground nutmeg or cinnamon.

◆ Instead of almond milk, try our Living Macadamia Milk (see page 185) or Living Cashew Milk (see page 187). They are all delicious.

Loving Living Granola

We love, love, love this protein-rich granola for breakfast, especially in the winter and spring. Don't forget to top each serving with fresh seasonal fruit and to add one of our delicious nut milks (see recipes beginning on page 185).

2 cups (504 g) uncooked steel-cut oats

1 tablespoon honey, or 2 tablespoons coconut sugar

1 cup (100 g) uncooked rolled oats

$^1/_2$ cup (70 g) chopped macadamia nuts

$^1/_2$ cup (72 g) sunflower seeds

$^1/_2$ cup (63 g) chopped walnuts

$^1/_2$ cup (56 g) slivered almonds

$^1/_2$ cup (38 g) shredded unsweetened coconut

$^1/_2$ cup (75 g) raisins

$^1/_2$ cup (85 g) dried cranberries

$^1/_3$ cup (38 g) sesame seeds

$^1/_3$ cup (33 g) hemp seeds

SERVINGS: 12   100% LIVING

1 Spread out the steel-cut oats on a dehydrator sheet and drizzle with honey. Dehydrate at 105°F (40°C) for approximately 8 hours, or until crisp and dry.

2 Break up the dried oats into a large bowl. Add all of the remaining ingredients and mix together well.

3 Divide the cereal among individual bowls, topping with your favorite nut milk, if desired.

4 Place leftovers in an airtight container and store in the pantry up to two months.

FOR A CHANGE

◆ If you have to avoid gluten, make sure that the oatmeal you buy is marked "gluten-free." Because of cross-contamination at the farm and in production facilities, most of the oatmeal you'll find on store shelves contains some gluten. To be safe, check the package label.

◆ To dry the cooked oats faster, place them in a low-temperature oven for about 1 hour. (See the inset on page 128.)

◆ Although this granola is delicious to enjoy as is, it's even better when topped with fresh seasonal fruit. We recommend fresh berries in the spring, stone fruits like peaches and apricots in the summer, chopped apples and pears in the fall and winter, and bananas all year round.

Breakfast Muesli

There are many variations of this classic cereal, which was created in the nineteenth century by Swiss doctor and nutritionist Maximilian Bircher-Benner. Consisting of grains, fruit, and nuts, muesli was considered the ideal nutritious breakfast.

1 cup (176 g) uncooked steel-cut or rolled oats

1 cup (237 ml) water

$^1/_2$ cup (75 g) raisins

$^1/_2$ cup (87 g) chopped pitted prunes

$^1/_2$ cup (75 g) chopped dried apricots

$^1/_2$ cup (62 g) grated apple

$^1/_4$ cup (28 g) slivered almonds

3 tablespoons honey or maple syrup

SERVINGS: 2   100% LIVING

1 Place all of the ingredients in a large bowl and mix together well. Cover and refrigerate 8 hours or overnight.

2 Remove the muesli about 1 hour before serving and let come to room temperature.

3 Divide the cereal among individual bowls, topping with fresh nut milk or fresh seasonal fruit.

FOR A CHANGE

◆ If you have to avoid gluten, make sure that the oatmeal you buy is marked "gluten-free." Because of cross-contamination at the farm and in production facilities, most of the oatmeal you'll find on store shelves contains some gluten. To be safe, check the package label.

If You Don't Have a Dehydrator . . .

Most of the beneficial enzymes in raw food are able to survive in temperatures below 115°F (46°C). The purpose of a dehydrator—basically an enclosed box that circulates warm air around raw food—is to "cook" the food with very low heat, which reduces the water content and preserves its natural enzymes. This appliance is commonly used to dehydrate fruits and vegetables, as well as "bake" items like breads, cookies, and crackers.

If you don't own a dehydrator, you can use your kitchen oven to achieve similar results. Simply set the oven on the lowest temperature setting and leave the door ajar as the food dehydrates. In most cases, food takes less time to dehydrate in the oven than in a dehydrator. If you use a convection oven, which constantly circulates the air, this process will take even less time than it would in a conventional oven.

Breakfast Muesli (see page 128).

Living Soups

We love our living soups! Along with being delicious and satisfying, they are great energy boosters. Enjoy them along with our super salads (beginning on page 97), or pair them with dishes that are cooked (see page 140) to bring greater "life" to the meal. We're betting that you and your family will love our living soups as much as we do.

Fresh Gazpacho

Vibrant and refreshing, this flavorful chilled soup makes the perfect light meal, especially on hot days. We also recommend pairing it with other dishes, like the Simple Walnut Rice Salad (see page 110), the Vegetarian Tacos (see page 149), and the Tofu Tacos (see page 150).

4 cups (1 L) fresh tomato juice (about 6 tomatoes)

3 cups (600 g) diced tomatoes

1 1/2 cups (225 g) peeled, diced cucumber

1/2 cup (88 g) diced green bell pepper

1/2 cup (13 g) chopped fresh cilantro

2 stalks celery, diced

2 avocados (preferably Haas), peeled and diced

5 cloves garlic, minced

2 tablespoons extra virgin olive oil

1 tablespoon fresh lemon juice

1/2 cup (50 g) chopped scallions (green onions) (for garnish)

SERVINGS: 4   100% LIVING

1 Place all of the ingredients except the scallions in a large bowl and mix together well.

2 Transfer half the mixture to a blender and blend until smooth. Return the blended mixture to the bowl and stir well.

3 Cover and refrigerate for 3 to 6 hours.

4 Divide the soup among individual soup bowls, and garnish with chopped scallions before serving.

Fresh Gazpacho (see page 130).

Make the Most of Your Soups

Whether preparing soups that are 100-percent living, partially cooked, or completely cooked, the following suggestions will help ensure that they are tasty and satisfying.

☐ For enhanced richness, add a drizzle of extra virgin olive oil, flax oil, or macadamia nut oil to the soup before serving.

☐ To thicken a watery soup, add some cooked brown rice or pearl barley. You can also mash some cooked beans (garbanzos are a good choice) to form a thick paste, then stir it into the soup. If your soup is living and you want to keep it that way, try puréeing a handful of cashews with a bit of the soup until creamy, and then return the soup to the pot; add a tablespoon or two of coconut oil; or blend in avocado, tahini, miso, or nut butters.

☐ Use your blender to adjust the consistency of your living or cooked soup. By simply changing the speed of your blender, you can make your soup thick, chunky, smooth—whatever you like.

☐ If adding bouillon, use only vegetable-based varieties.

☐ To give cooked soups a "beefy" taste, add mushrooms—whole or sliced.

☐ Enhance the flavor of soups with herbs and spices—fresh or dried. Herbs like rosemary, oregano, and thyme are especially welcome in hearty vegetable and tomato-based soups, while light brothy soups may benefit from a handful of chopped scallions, chives, or minced parsley. To make spicy soups even spicier, add a little minced hot chili pepper. And don't forget about garlic, which goes with nearly everything!

☐ Be careful not to oversalt your vegetable-based soup during its preparation. As this type of soup sits, the natural sodium from the vegetables will give it a salty flavor.

☐ For increased visual appeal, add garnishes to the soup before serving. Chopped scallions, sprigs of parsley and cilantro, fresh basil and mint leaves, and chopped chives are a few popular choices. For crunch, sprinkle on some sesame, hemp, pumpkin, or sunflower seeds. Another great topping is grated or spiralized zucchini, cucumber, carrot, or jicama.

☐ After preparing your soup, if you have time, it is best to let it to sit in the refrigerator for a few hours before serving. This allows the flavors to blend and become more intense. Even a fifteen-minute stay in the fridge will make your soup much more tasty. Most cooked soups store well for two or three days, but if your soup is living, to avoid bacterial growth, you'll want to refrigerate it for no more than ten hours before eating.

☐ Most soups freeze well. Before freezing, portion the soup in individual serving containers, which make for quick and easy thawing.

Ruby Red Ambrosia Living Soup

This is a wonderful "cleansing" soup (especially for the liver). Enjoy it with your favorite whole grain bread.

2 medium-sized vine-ripened tomatoes, cut into chunks

$\frac{1}{2}$ medium-sized beet

$\frac{1}{3}$ medium-sized yellow onion, cut into chunks

1-inch piece fresh ginger, peeled

1 clove garlic

$\frac{1}{2}$ cup (118 ml) fresh lime juice

2 tablespoons tahini

2 tablespoons chopped fresh basil

$\frac{1}{3}$ teaspoon celery salt

Sea salt and black pepper to taste

$\frac{1}{2}$ large unwaxed cucumber, coarsely chopped

SERVINGS: 2   100% LIVING

1 Place all of the ingredients except the cucumber in a blender. Pulse or blend to the desired consistency.

2 Add the cucumber and continue to pulse to the desired thickness.

3 Divide the soup among individual bowls, and serve.

Mango Salsa Living Soup

This delicious mango-sweetened soup comes with a flavorful spark of heat. Pair it with any of our super salads—the Simple Walnut Rice Salad (see page 110) and the Millet Basil Salad (see page 111) are especially good choices.

8 medium-sized carrots, coarsely chopped

2 avocados (preferably Haas), peeled and cut into chunks

1 cucumber, peeled and coarsely chopped

1 medium-sized vine-ripened tomato, cut into chunks

1 teaspoon ground cumin

$1/8$ teaspoon cayenne pepper, or 1-inch square fresh jalapeño pepper

1 large mango, peeled and cut into small pieces

$1/2$ medium-sized red bell pepper, diced

1 clove garlic, crushed

3–4 tablespoons chopped fresh cilantro

$1 1/2$ tablespoons chopped fresh basil

2 tablespoons diced sweet onion

2 tablespoons fresh lime juice

Sea salt and black pepper to taste

SERVINGS: 2   100% LIVING

1 Place the carrots, avocados, cucumber, tomato, cumin, and cayenne pepper in a blender. Pulse or blend to the desired consistency (we prefer it chunky).

2 Transfer the mixture to a large bowl, and stir in the mango, red pepper, garlic, cilantro, basil, onion, and lime juice. Stir well, and add salt and black pepper to taste.

3 Divide the soup among individual bowls, and serve.

A Word About Avocados

Rich in beneficial monounsaturated fats, avocados are also a wonderful source of essential nutrients, including fiber, potassium, vitamin E, and B vitamins. Although there are many varieties of this fruit (yes, it's a fruit), the two most popular are the Haas (California) and the Fuerte (Florida) avocados. Unlike the smooth, thin-skinned green Fuerte, Haas varieties have a rough outer skin that ranges in color from dark green to black. In terms of flavor and texture, Haas avocados have a richer, more buttery taste and a smoother, creamier texture—they are the ones we recommend for our recipes.

Jay's Quick Energy Soup

Super easy to prepare, this cleansing, energy-boosting soup tastes fantastic. One of our summertime favorites, we usually serve it with the Basic Soba Noodle Salad (see page 88).

8 medium-sized carrots, coarsely chopped

$1/2$ small beet, cut in half

1 avocado (preferably Haas), peeled and cut into chunks

$1/2$ teaspoon ground cumin

$1/8$ teaspoon cayenne pepper, or 1-inch square fresh jalapeño pepper

Sea salt and black pepper to taste

Chopped tomatoes, scallions, pumpkin seeds, and cilantro (for garnish)

SERVINGS: 4   100% LIVING

1 Place all of the ingredients, except for the garnish options, in a blender. Pulse or blend to the desired consistency.

2 Divide the soup among individual bowls, and garnish with the tomatoes, scallions, and cilantro before serving.

Removing the pit and skin from a ripe avocado is a fairly simple process. Just follow these three easy steps:

1. Cut the avocado in half lengthwise around the pit with a sharp knife. Twist the halves to separate.

2. To remove the pit, choose one of the following popular methods. Gently slide the tip of a spoon beneath the pit and lift it out. Or give the pit a firm but quick chop with a sharp knife (the knife will partially penetrate the pit), then twist the knife to easily remove the pit.

3. Scoop the avocado from the skin with a spoon.

You can store ripe uncut avocados in the refrigerator for two or three days. Once they have been cut, sprinkle with a little lemon or lime juice (to prevent browning), and refrigerate in an airtight container.

Cleansing Living Soup

Along with the Digestive Juice Aids offered on pages 164 to 169, we recommend this soup any time you want to heal and detoxify your body.

1 large green zucchini, coarsely chopped

1 medium-sized red bell pepper, coarsely chopped

1 avocado (preferably Haas), peeled and cut into chunks

1 1/2 cups (355 ml) water

1 cup (25 g) chopped fresh parsley

1 cup (25 g) chopped fresh cilantro

3 tablespoons white miso

2 tablespoons tamari or Bragg Liquid Aminos

1/4 teaspoon cayenne pepper

Chopped tomatoes, scallions (green onions), and cilantro (for garnish)

Crushed toasted nori (for garnish)

SERVINGS: 2   100% LIVING

1 Place all of the ingredients except the garnish options in a blender. Pulse or blend to the desired consistency.

2 Divide the soup among individual soup bowls, and garnish with the tomatoes, scallions, cilantro, and a sprinkling of toasted nori before serving.

FOR A CHANGE

◆ If you have to avoid gluten, be sure to buy a gluten-free brand of tamari or to use Bragg Liquid Aminos, which is gluten-free. Also make sure that your miso is marked "gluten-free."

Lovely and Luscious Living Soup

This is Linda's favorite soup, and it takes only minutes to prepare. Enjoy a bowl along with a wrap that's filled with our Super Salad with Black Beans (see page 108).

1 cup (75 g) fresh spinach

1 cup (237 ml) water

2 medium-sized vine-ripened tomatoes, cut into chunks

2 cloves garlic

2 tablespoons tahini

1 teaspoon white miso

1 teaspoon sea salt

1 teaspoon black pepper

SERVINGS: 2   **100% LIVING**

1 Place all of the ingredients in a blender. Pulse or blend to the desired consistency.

2 Divide the soup among individual bowls, and serve.

FOR A CHANGE

◆ If you have to avoid gluten, make sure that the miso is marked "gluten-free." Miso can be made with gluten, so it's important to check the label.

Jay's Magic Living Soup

Why is this magic soup? Because every time we make it, it disappears! Goes great with our Basic Salad (see page 85).

12 medium-sized carrots

$^1/_2$ lime, unpeeled

2-inch piece fresh ginger, peeled

1 pound (454 g) soft tofu

3 cloves garlic

2 tablespoons tahini

2 tablespoons tamari or Bragg Liquid Aminos

$^1/_2$ teaspoon black pepper

1 medium-sized zucchini, julienned

2 stalks celery, chopped

1 tomato, diced

$^1/_2$ cup (13 g) minced fresh cilantro

2 tablepoons minced fresh parsley

Sea salt to taste

SERVINGS: 4–6   **80% LIVING**

1 Juice the carrots with the lime and ginger.

2 Transfer the juice to a blender along with the tofu, garlic, tahini, tamari, and black pepper. Blend until smooth.

3 Pour the mixture into a large bowl. Add the zucchini, celery, tomato, cilantro, and parsley, and stir until well blended. Add sea salt to taste. Cover and refrigerate for 1 to 2 hours.

4 Divide the soup among individual bowls, and serve.

FOR A CHANGE

◆ If you have to avoid gluten, be sure to buy a gluten-free brand of tamari or to use Bragg Liquid Aminos, which is gluten-free.

◆ For greater texture, reserve some of the carrot pulp after juicing, and stir it into the finished soup.

Cooked Choices

Certain cooked foods—including whole grains, vegetables, and beans—can be wholesome and nourishing when eaten with a combination of predominantly living foods. For instance, along with Miso Healing Soup, found on page 145, consider serving our Basic Salad (see page 85). A glass of one of our many digestive aids (see page 164) can also add more living foods to your menu while helping your body more easily digest the cooked ingredients. The wide range of living recipes offered in this book will make it easy to vary the dishes you serve alongside the following cooked choices.

Carrot-Ginger Soup

Enjoy this flavorful soup with any of our living super salads. It also pairs well with Green Power Tummy Remedy juice (see page 166).

12 cups (3 L) water

10 medium-sized carrots, finely diced or thinly sliced

1 medium-sized leek, cleaned and cut into 1-inch slices

1-inch piece fresh ginger, peeled and finely chopped

1 $1/2$ teaspoons ground nutmeg

1 teaspoon sea salt

$1/2$ teaspoon black pepper

Chopped scallions (green onions) (for garnish)

SERVINGS: 4   0% LIVING

1 Place all of the ingredients except the scallions in a large pot and place over medium-high heat. As soon as it comes to a gentle boil, reduce the heat to low and gently simmer for 20 minutes, or until the carrots are soft.

2 Transfer the mixture to a blender, and blend to the desired consistency. (This may have to be done in two or three batches.)

3 Garnish with chopped scallions and serve.

FOR A CHANGE

◆ For an added burst of flavor, before serving, add a spoonful of Our Favorite Simple Salsa (see page 205) and top with avocado slices and chopped parsley.

Nutty Rice and Veggies

This nutritious brown rice dish features a variety of wonderful tastes and textures. Accompany it with our Basic Salad (see page 85) for a healthy, satisfying meal.

1 ¹/₂ cups (173 g) sunflower seeds

1 cup (112 g) slivered almonds

3 carrots, julienned

2 stalks celery, chopped

1 yellow or red bell pepper, chopped

2 cups (200 g) chopped scallions (green onions)

¹/₂ cup (75 g) diced yellow onions

¹/₂ cup (75 g) raisins

Black or cayenne pepper to taste

4 cups (1 kg) hot cooked short-grain brown rice

2 tablespoons extra virgin olive oil

2 avocados (preferably Haas), peeled, pitted, and sliced (for garnish)

1 large tomato, chopped (for garnish)

¹/₂ cup (70 g) pitted black olives (for garnish)

SERVINGS: 4   **60–75% LIVING**

1 Preheat the oven to 300°F.

2 Place the sunflower seeds and almonds in an ovenproof bowl. Add the carrots, celery, bell pepper, scallions, onions, raisins, and black pepper, and stir to combine. Cover the ingredients with the hot brown rice.

3 Place the bowl in the oven for 15 minutes or until the ingredients are heated through. Add the olive oil and toss well.

4 Garnish individual portions with avocado slices, chopped tomatoes, and olives before serving.

FOR A CHANGE

◆ To add even more living ingredients to this dish, use additional toppings, such as fresh sprouts and julienned raw zucchini and beets.

Asian Green Beans

Our Millet Basil Salad (see page 111) pairs well with these garlicky ginger-flavored green beans. To make your meal more "alive," also serve these dishes with a glass of Popeye's Digestive Special (see page 168).

2 cups (300 g) diagonally cut French green beans

1 tablespoon extra virgin olive oil

1 teaspoon sesame oil

2 cloves garlic, crushed

1-inch piece fresh ginger, peeled and finely chopped

2 tablespoons tamari or Bragg Liquid Aminos

SERVINGS: 4   0% LIVING

1 Steam the beans in a bamboo or stainless steel steamer for about 5 minutes, or until they turn bright green and are tender-crisp (al dente). Transfer the beans to a serving bowl and set aside.

2 While the beans are cooking, place the olive oil, sesame oil, garlic, and ginger in a small pot over medium-low heat. Heat for 2 or 3 minutes or until the garlic starts to become aromatic. Add the tamari. Continue to heat another minute.

3 Pour the garlic-ginger oil over the warm beans, toss, and serve.

FOR A CHANGE

◆ If you have to avoid gluten, be sure to buy a gluten-free brand of tamari or to use Bragg Liquid Aminos, which is gluten-free.

Carrot-Ginger Soup (see page 140).

Super-Easy Broccoli Soup

This recipe is so easy to prepare and very filling! The coconut oil adds a creamy richness, making it a great choice for those who love "cream" soups but are lactose intolerant. We suggest serving it with our Basic Salad (see page 85) and a glass of Heavy-Duty Green Digestive (see page 166) to give your meal an enzyme boost.

2 cups (474 ml) water

1 cube vegetable bouillon

3 cups (525 g) chopped broccoli (including stems)

3 cloves garlic

1 $\frac{1}{2}$ tablespoons coconut oil

Sea salt to taste

Black pepper to taste

SERVINGS: 2–4   0% LIVING

1 Place the water, bouillon, broccoli, and garlic in a pot over medium-low heat. Cover and simmer gently for 15 to 20 minutes, or until the broccoli is tender.

2 Transfer the broccoli and cooking liquid to a blender along with the coconut oil. Blend until smooth and creamy. Taste the soup, and season to taste with salt and pepper.

3 Serve immediately.

FOR A CHANGE

◆ If you have to avoid gluten, make sure that the vegetable bouillon you use is marked "gluten-free."

◆ For added "kick," instead of black pepper, flavor this soup with a sprinkling of cayenne pepper.

Miso Healing Soup

In need of a little tender loving care? Look no further than this comforting, nutrient-rich soup that spotlights miso—a Japanese staple that has long been known for its healing properties and role in maintaining good health. Enjoy it with our Basic Salad (see page 85).

12 cups (3 L) water

12 x 4-inch strip kombu sea vegetable

$^1/_2$ cup (75g) julienned carrots

1 cup (75 g) sliced oyster mushrooms

3 cups (300 g) shredded napa or savoy cabbage

2 cups (180 g) watercress

1 $^1/_2$ cups (338 g) dark miso

1 pound (454 g) firm tofu, cubed

1 cup (100 g) chopped scallions (green onions) (for garnish)

SERVINGS: 4–6   0% LIVING

1 Place the water and kombu in a large pot and bring to a boil. Remove the kombu, cut it into long strips, and return it to the pot.

2 Add the carrots and mushrooms to the pot, and gently boil for about 6 minutes. Add the cabbage, and cook for an additional 4 minutes, or until the vegetables are tender. Reduce the heat to low, add the watercress, and simmer gently.

3 Place the miso in a fine-screened strainer. Immerse the bottom of the strainer in the simmering soup to soften the miso. With the back of a wooden spoon, push the softened miso through the strainer into the pot.

4 Add the tofu cubes to the pot, and simmer another minute or until the tofu is warm.

5 Ladle the soup into bowls, garnish with scallions, and serve.

FOR A CHANGE

◆ For added flavor, texture, and nutritional value, add a spoonful of brown rice to the individual servings.

◆ If you have to avoid gluten, make sure the miso you use is marked "gluten-free."

Veggie Wraps with Thai Peanut Sauce

These hearty wraps are filled with a delicious combination of beans, grains, and veggies that are tossed with a 100-percent living spicy peanut sauce. Because these wraps are a bit heavy, we recommend enjoying them with our Basic Digestive Tonic (see page 164).

2 large red potatoes, cut into bite-sized cubes

3 carrots, julienned

1 small cauliflower, chopped into florets

2 cups (500 g) cooked short-grain brown rice

2 cups (468 g) cooked black beans

4 (14-inch) spinach or basil tortillas

2 cups (150 g) chopped romaine lettuce

1 cup (33 g) alfalfa or sunflower sprouts (see page 102 for sprouting instructions)

1 cup (25 g) chopped cilantro

Thai Peanut Sauce

$1/2$ cup (118 ml) fresh lime juice

6 tablespoons creamy peanut butter (not hydrogenated or roasted)

6 tablespoons tamari or Bragg Liquid aminos

6 tablespoons honey

4 tablespoons chili paste

8 cloves garlic, minced

SERVINGS: 4   25% LIVING

1 Steam the potatoes in a bamboo or stainless steel steamer for 10 to 15 minutes, or until the cubes begin to soften. Add the carrots and cauliflower, and continue to steam for another 8 minutes, or until tender. Remove from the heat, cover, and let sit for another 5 minutes.

2 While the vegetables are steaming, place all of the sauce ingredients in a blender, and pulse or blend to the desired consistency. Set aside.

3 Transfer the steamed vegetables to a large mixing bowl, and stir in the rice and beans. Set aside.

4 Warm the tortillas in a toaster oven or dry skillet (so they can fold without breaking).

5 Arrange equal portions of the vegetable-rice mixture on each warm tortilla, leaving a 2- to 3-inch border around the edge (or the filling will seep out). Top with lettuce, sprouts, and cilantro.

6 Fold the right and left sides of each tortilla over the filling. Then, starting from the bottom, roll them up. Place seam-side down on the plate.

7 Top the wraps with a liberal amount of peanut sauce, and serve.

◆ Enjoy the very versatile Thai Peanut Sauce—which yields about 2 cups—with lots of other foods. Spoon some over Asian Green Beans (see page 142), add a drizzle to our living soups, or use it as a dip for raw veggies.

◆ If you have to avoid gluten, be sure to buy a gluten-free brand of tamari or to use Bragg Liquid Aminos, which is gluten-free. Also be sure to use gluten-free tortillas.

Perfect Pita Sandwich

Although we avoid most baked bread, we occasionally use yeast-free pita rounds. (Yeast has been implicated in a number of digestive problems.) This sandwich is a favorite among adults and kids alike. We often serve it with Jay's Beet-Apple Salad (see page 113) and a glass of Digestive Calming Tonic (see page 165).

2 cups (460 g) Homemade Hummus (see page 208)

4 yeast-free whole grain pita rounds

1 avocado (preferably Haas), mashed

1 zucchini, julienned

1 carrot, julienned

2 cups (150 g) chopped romaine lettuce

3 scallions (green onions), chopped

2 tomatoes, chopped

SERVINGS: 4   **50–60% LIVING**

1 Spread a generous layer of hummus into each pita pocket, and top with 1 or 2 spoonfuls of avocado.

2 Add the zucchini, carrots, romaine lettuce, scallions, and tomatoes to each pita.

3 Serve immediately.

FOR A CHANGE

◆ For added flavor, spoon some Tofu Tarragon Tomato Dressing (see page 115) over the filling before serving.

◆ If you have to avoid gluten, make sure to use a bread that's marked "gluten-free."

Lentil Burgers

After many years of experimenting, we came up with these terrific-tasting burgers. Garnish them with lots of living foods like tomatoes, onions, lettuce, sprouts, and shredded veggies. As these burgers are mostly cooked, it's a good idea to accompany them with a glass of enzyme-rich Salad Tonic Digestive (see page 169).

2 stalks celery, diced

$\frac{1}{2}$ medium onion, diced

$\frac{1}{2}$ cup (13 g) finely chopped parsley

2 cloves garlic, crushed

$1\frac{1}{2}$ cups (150 g) uncooked rolled oats

$\frac{1}{2}$ cup (45 g) breadcrumbs

$\frac{1}{2}$ cup (125 g) mashed pinto beans

1 cup (75 g) cooked lentils

1 tablespoon almond butter

1 tablespoon tamari or Bragg Liquid Aminos

Sea salt and black pepper to taste

SERVINGS: 4–6   0% LIVING

1 Preheat the oven to 350°F.

2 Place all of the ingredients in a large bowl, and mix until well combined.

3 Oil a baking sheet with macadamia or coconut oil. With oiled hands, form the lentil mixture into 4 to 6 patties, and place on the prepared sheet.

4 Bake about 20 minutes on each side or until golden brown.

5 Serve each burger on a bun, top with sliced tomatoes and other living foods, or place each one atop one of our living salads.

FOR A CHANGE

◆ If you have to avoid gluten, be sure to buy a gluten-free brand of tamari or to use Bragg Liquid Aminos, which is gluten-free. Also make sure that the breadcrumbs and oatmeal you buy is marked "gluten-free." Because of cross-contamination at the farm and in production facilities, most of the oatmeal you'll find on store shelves contains some gluten. To be safe, check the package label.

◆ Try these burgers stuffed inside yeast-free whole wheat pita pockets instead of the usual bun.

◆ For added moistness, top the burgers with a drizzle of Superfast Tahini Dressing (see page 117).

Vegetarian Tacos

These delicious, satisfying tacos are an especially good choice for people who have wheat allergies or are gluten intolerant. A glass of Meal Sipper Digestive (see page 167) will complete the meal.

1 3/4 cups (414 ml) water

1 cup (145 g) uncooked millet

2 avocados (preferably Haas), mashed

1 cup (150 g) diced onion

1 cup (140 g) diced olives

1/4 cup (59 ml) tamari or Bragg Liquid Aminos

8 corn tortillas

1 cup (75 g) chopped romaine lettuce

1 cup (200 g) chopped tomatoes

1 cup (175 g) julienned or grated zucchini

1 cup (150 g) julienned or grated carrots

1/4 cup Our Favorite Simple Salsa (see page 205)

SERVINGS: 4 (2 TACOS EACH) 75 % LIVING

1 Place the water in a small pot and bring to a boil over medium-high heat. Add the millet, stir once, and reduce the heat to low. Cover and simmer for 30 minutes or until the millet is tender. Set aside to cool for 10 minutes.

2 Add the avocados, onions, olives, and tamari to the cooked millet. Stir until well combined.

3 Warm the tortillas in a toaster oven or dry skillet (so they can fold without breaking).

4 Place equal portions of the millet mixture on each warm tortilla; then top with the remaining ingredients. Fold the tortillas in half and serve.

FOR A CHANGE

◆ Before serving these tacos, add a flavorful scoop of creamy Homemade Hummus (see page 203).

◆ Instead of salsa, try these tacos with a heaping spoonful of Superfast Tahini Dressing (see page 117) or Super Green Salad Dressing (see page 120).

◆ If you have to avoid gluten, be sure to buy a gluten-free brand of tamari or to use Bragg Liquid Aminos, which is gluten-free. Also be sure to buy tortillas that are marked "gluten-free."

Tofu Tacos

We often serve these delicious tacos with bowls of Fresh Gazpacho (see page 130) and glasses of Three "C's" Digestive Juice (see page 169).

12 ounces (340 g) firm tofu

2 tablespoons tamari or Bragg Liquid Aminos

1 tablespoon fresh lime juice

1 1/2 teaspoons chili powder

1 teaspoon garlic powder

1 teaspoon ground cumin

1/4 teaspoon cayenne pepper

3 cups (300 g) shredded cabbage

2 cups (350 g) julienned zucchini

1/4 cup (25 g) chopped scallions (green onions)

2 cups alfalfa sprouts (see page 102 for sprouting instructions)

8 corn tortillas

1 cup (226 g) Our Favorite Simple Salsa (see page 205)

SERVINGS: 4 (2 TACOS EACH)   **75% LIVING**

1 Preheat the oven to 400°F.

2 Rinse the tofu and drain in a colander for a few minutes; then pat dry with paper towels. While the tofu is draining, oil a baking sheet with macadamia nut or coconut oil. Cut the tofu into 1–inch cubes, lightly blot with more paper towels, and place on the prepared baking sheet.

3 Bake the tofu about 20 minutes or until browned.

4 While the tofu is browning, place the tamari, lime juice, chili powder, garlic powder, cumin, and cayenne pepper in a large bowl and mix well. Add the tofu, and gently stir to coat. Let stand 5 minutes.

5 In a separate bowl, toss together the cabbage, zucchini, scallions, and alfalfa sprouts. Set aside.

6 Warm the tortillas in a toaster oven or dry skillet (so they can fold without breaking).

7 Place equal portions of tofu on each warm tortilla. Add the cabbage-zucchini mixture, and top with the salsa. Fold the tortillas in half and serve.

FOR A CHANGE

◆ If you have to avoid gluten, be sure to buy a gluten-free brand of tamari or to use Bragg Liquid Aminos, which is gluten-free. Also be sure to use tortillas that are marked "gluten-free."

◆ Before adding the filling ingredients, spread the tortillas with a layer of Homemade Hummus (see page 203).

Whole World Tostadas

These easy-to-prepare tostadas are satisfying and delicious, and can be enjoyed as complete meals. They are also visually beautiful! Try them with our Basic Digestive Tonic (see page 164).

4 (12-inch) spinach tortillas

2 $1/2$ cups (585 g) cooked black beans

$1/2$ cup (75 g) diced onions

1 cup (75 g) chopped romaine lettuce

1 cup (100 g) shredded green cabbage

1 cup (150 g) grated or julienned carrots

1 cup (150 g) julienned green zucchini

$1/2$ cup (13 g) chopped fresh cilantro

$1/2$ cup (13 g) chopped fresh parsley

1 cup (237 g) Super-Simple Guacamole (see page 204)

$1/2$ cup (68 g) sliced olives

1 cup (226 g) Our Favorite Simple Salsa (see page 205)

SERVINGS: 4　　　**50–75% LIVING**

1 Heat the tortillas in a dry skillet over medium heat until they begin to bubble and become somewhat crisp. (Be careful not to burn.)

2 While the tortillas are heating up, warm the beans in a pot over low heat.

3 On each crisp tortilla, layer equal portions of the ingredients in the following order:

- black beans
- onions
- lettuce and cabbage
- carrots and zucchini
- cilantro and parsley
- guacamole and olives
- salsa

4 Serve immediately.

FOR A CHANGE

◆ If you have to avoid gluten, make sure that the tortillas you use are marked "gluten-free."

◆ If you prefer a thicker base for your tostadas, use two tortillas instead of one.

Juice Therapy Recipes

Throughout this book, we discuss how freshly made vegetable and fruit juices can deliciously provide you with abundant energy and vibrant good health. Fresh juice is the ultimate food for your body—predigested and 100-percent absorbable. This chapter offers a wide range of great juice recipes.

The chapter is divided into four sections. It begins with our "Top Vitality Juices," each of which not only boosts energy but also supports particular body functions. Then you'll find our "Digestive Juice Aids," which were specifically designed to aid the digestion of cooked foods—and, of course, to relieve stomach ailments—but are great with living foods, as well. Following this, we have "Juices for Kids." Milder in flavor than our other juices, these combinations are sure to win over any child to the juicing lifestyle! Finally, you'll find "Jay's Healing Juices." These are classic combinations he has been using for over six decades to enhance organ health, promote longevity, and improve physical condition.

> **"Your health, happiness, and the future of life on earth are rarely so much in your own hands as when you sit down to eat."**
>
> **—John Robbins, Author**

Tips for Juicing Success

Juicing is truly easy. It involves no complicated techniques and, of course, no cooking. Nevertheless, you'll enjoy the most delicious and healthful results if you follow a few simple rules for selecting, preparing, and juicing your fresh produce.

☐ To optimize both taste and nutrients, choose only the freshest, best-quality produce available. If at all possible, buy organic fruits and veggies.

☐ Prior to juicing, clean your produce just as you would if you were preparing a salad or steamed vegetables. Thoroughly wash all produce in water, and use a vegetable brush to scrub veggies like carrots and beets. As a rule, except for a few fruits discussed below, you should leave the peel on your fruit.

☐ Peel pineapple, kiwi, and any other produce whose peel can impart a bitter flavor to your juice. When juicing oranges, grapefruits, and tangerines, remove the peel, but leave on most of the nutrient-rich white pith. Lemons and limes, however, should be juiced with the peel still on.

☐ Choose unwaxed cucumbers—the long, narrow ones that come wrapped in plastic—so that you don't have to remove the peel before you juice them. They may be referred to as *seedless cucumbers, hothouse cucumbers, or English cucumbers*.

☐ Remove and discard apple cores as well as any large seeds and pits. (Note that apple seeds contain small amounts of toxic substances.)

☐ Remove any bruised areas of your produce, any leaves that have become discolored, and any greens that have a bitter taste.

☐ Cut your produce into pieces that are small enough to accommodate the feeding tube of your juicer.

☐ Some fruits—papayas and bananas, for instance—are hard to juice because they are very fibrous or contain relatively little water. Some berries fall into this category, as well. Pureé these fruits in a blender—along with the juice from the other ingredients—instead of juicing them.

☐ Follow each recipe's directions for feeding the different ingredients through your juicer. To make sure that greens and herbs end up in your juice rather than stuck to the machine, bunch them up tightly when feeding them through. Never juice leafy greens or herbs last. Instead, follow them with ingredients like carrots or apples, which will flush any remaining greens into the juicer's bowl.

TOP VITALITY JUICES

Apple Beet Juice

This combination of apples and raw beets provides effective cleansing for the liver.

4 Golden Delicious apples, cored and quartered

1 beet with greens, quartered

SERVINGS: 2   100% LIVING

1 Alternately juice the apples and beets until all the ingredients are juiced.

2 Pour into individual glasses and serve.

Apple and Celery Juice

After a workout, this refreshing combination replaces lost fluids and nutrients.

4 Golden Delicious apples, cored and quartered

6 stalks celery

SERVINGS: 2   100% LIVING

1 Alternately juice the apples and celery until all the ingredients are juiced.

2 Pour into individual glasses and serve.

Apple and Pear Juice

Here is a delicious, totally natural way to relieve constipation. For best results, drink it at bedtime.

4 Golden Delicious apples, cored and quartered

2 firm pears, cored and quartered

SERVINGS: 2　　**100% LIVING**

1 Alternately juice the apples and pears until all the ingredients are juiced.

2 Pour into individual glasses and serve.

Carrot, Cucumber, and Cabbage Juice

Cabbage and cucumbers relieve stomach problems and cleanse the kidneys, while carrots ensure great taste.

12 medium-sized carrots, trimmed

1/4 head green cabbage, cut into chunks

1 large unwaxed cucumber, quartered

SERVINGS: 4　　**100% LIVING**

1 Alternately juice 6 of the carrots and all of the cabbage and cucumber. Finish by juicing the remaining carrots.

2 Pour into individual glasses and serve.

Jay's Anti-Cancer Tonic (page 162).

Pineapple and Apple Juice

This delicious combination boosts energy and does wonders to ease the pain of arthritis. For more powerful but stronger-tasting arthritis relief, see Arthur-itis Helper on page 179.

³/₄-inch piece fresh ginger, peeled

3 Golden Delicious apples, cored and quartered

¹/₂ pineapple, peeled and cut into spears

SERVINGS: 4   100% LIVING

1 Juice the ginger. Then alternately juice the apples and pineapple until all the ingredients are juiced.

2 Pour into individual glasses and serve.

Carrot and Cantaloupe Juice

Extremely high in antioxidants, this beverage provides a pleasant way to improve your complexion. Although we usually don't combine vegetables with any fruit other than apples, in this case, the combination is easy to digest and loaded with nutrients.

8 medium-sized carrots, trimmed

¹/₂ cantaloupe, cut into chunks

SERVINGS: 2   100% LIVING

1 Alternately juice the carrots and cantaloupe until all the ingredients are juiced.

2 Pour into individual glasses and serve.

FOR A CHANGE

◆ For a change of pace, substitute a medium-sized sweet potato for the cantaloupe.

Left: Carrot and Cantaloupe Juice (see page 158).
Center Back: Pineapple and Apple Juice (see page 158).
Right: Jay's Famous Lemonade (see page 171).

Watermelon Juice (see page 161).

The Carrots and Greens Machine

A nutrient-packed combination, this juice aids digestion, benefits the kidneys, and improves eye health.

8 medium-sized carrots, trimmed

Handful curly endive

Handful kale

1 large unwaxed cucumber, quartered

SERVINGS: 3　　　100% LIVING

1 Alternately juice 4 of the carrots and all of the endive and kale, tightly bunching up the greens as you feed them through the machine. Juice the cucumber, and finish by juicing the remaining carrots.

2 Pour into individual glasses and serve.

Watermelon Juice

In addition to being tasty, watermelon enhances kidney function and replaces lost fluids. If you want to include the rind, you must buy organic fruit. If you simply can't find organic watermelon, juice only the flesh. Double or triple this recipe if you have kids. They love this pink drink!

1-inch-thick slice watermelon, cut into long spears

SERVINGS: 1　　　100% LIVING

1 Juice the spears of watermelon.

2 Pour into a glass and serve.

Carrot and Coconut Juice

This super-tonic makes a perfect breakfast, but can also help you relax in the evening. High in nutrients, including essential fatty acids, this beverage supports beautiful skin and hair, and also strengthens cardiovascular health.

14 medium-sized carrots, trimmed

1 baby coconut and its liquid*

* See page 91 for preparation instructions.

SERVINGS: 3　　　**100% LIVING**

1 Juice the carrots.

2 Transfer the carrot juice to a blender, and add the meat and liquid of the coconut. Blend until smooth and well combined.

3 Pour into individual glasses and serve.

FOR A CHANGE

◆ To spice things up, juice a 1-inch piece of raw ginger along with the carrots.

Jay's Anti-Cancer Tonic

This tonic is based on Dr. Gerson's simple but effective anti-cancer juice.

6 medium-sized carrots, trimmed

2 Golden Delicious apples, cored and quartered

SERVINGS: 2　　　**100% LIVING**

1 Alternately juice the carrots and apples until all the ingredients are juiced.

2 Pour into individual glasses and serve.

Left: Heavy-Duty Green Digestive (see page 166).
Center: Salad Tonic Digestive (see page 169).
Right: Green Tummy Machine (see page 167).

Basic Digestive Tonic

This delicious combination not only aids digestion but also acts as a diuretic to eliminate excess fluids from the body when you've had too much salt.

8 medium-sized carrots, trimmed

Handful spinach

2 stalks celery

SERVINGS: 2   100% LIVING

1 Alternately juice 4 of the carrots and all of the spinach, tightly bunching up the spinach as you feed it through the machine. Juice the celery, and finish by juicing the remaining carrots.

2 Pour into individual glasses and serve.

Blood-Building Digestive

In addition to relieving stomach problems, this juice boosts iron intake and cleanses the blood.

8 medium-sized carrots, trimmed

3 large kale leaves

Handful spinach

SERVINGS: 2   100% LIVING

1 Alternatively juice 4 of the carrots and all of the kale and spinach, tightly bunching up the greens as you feed them through the machine. Finish by juicing the remaining carrots.

2 Pour into individual glasses and serve.

Digestive Calming Tonic

A wonderful aid to the digestion of cooked foods, this tonic is also a great bedtime beverage when you're feeling stressed.

8 medium-sized carrots, trimmed

Handful spinach

Handful fresh parsley

2 stalks celery

SERVINGS: 2   100% LIVING

1 Alternately juice 4 of the carrots and all of the spinach and parsley, tightly bunching up the greens as you feed them through the machine. Juice the celery, and finish by juicing the remaining carrots.

2 Pour into individual glasses and serve.

Digestive Companion

This is an effective remedy for both diarrhea and constipation.

8 medium-sized carrots, trimmed

Handful spinach

SERVINGS: 1   100% LIVING

1 Alternately juice 4 of the carrots and all of the spinach, tightly bunching up the spinach as you feed it through the machine. Finish by juicing the remaining carrots.

2 Pour into a glass and serve.

Heavy-Duty Green Digestive

A strong digestive tonic, this combination of carrots and green veggies is the perfect accompaniment to a Chinese entrée or any difficult-to-digest meal.

8 medium-sized carrots, trimmed

3 large leaves bok choy (Chinese cabbage)

Handful spinach

6 medium-sized broccoli florets

SERVINGS: 2   100% LIVING

1 Alternatively juice 4 of the carrots with the bok choy and spinach, tightly bunching up the greens as you feed them through the machine. Juice the broccoli, and finish by juicing the remaining carrots.

2 Pour into individual glasses and serve.

Green Power Tummy Remedy

Perfect for stomachaches caused by overeating, this tonic's flavor and effectiveness are enhanced by ginger root, a powerful digestive aid.

8 medium-sized carrots, trimmed

Handful fresh parsley

Handful spinach

2 stalks celery

$1/2$-inch piece fresh ginger, peeled

SERVINGS: 2   100% LIVING

1 Alternately juice 4 of the carrots and all of the parsley and spinach, tightly bunching up the greens as you feed them through the machine. Juice the celery, followed by the ginger. Finish with the remaining carrots.

2 Pour into individual glasses and serve.

Green Tummy Machine

This is the king of digestive remedies. Use it to relieve all types of indigestion, including heartburn.

1 large unwaxed cucumber, quartered

Handful kale

Handful spinach

Handful parsley

1 lime, rind included, halved

2-inch-thick wedge green cabbage, cut into chunks

4 stalks celery

SERVINGS: 2   100% LIVING

1 Alternately juice the cucumber with the kale, spinach, and parsley, tightly bunching up the greens as you feed them through the machine. Then juice the lime followed by the cabbage and celery,

2 Pour into individual glasses and serve.

Meal Sipper Digestive

Sip this tasty tonic with your meal to avoid digestive upset.

6–8 medium-sized carrots, trimmed

Handful spinach

SERVINGS: 1   100% LIVING

1 Alternately juice half of the carrots and all of the spinach, tightly bunching up the spinach as you feed it through the machine. Finish by juicing the remaining carrots.

2 Pour into a glass and serve.

Popeye's Digestive Special

Packed with iron, this tonic also promotes the digestion of cooked foods and cleanses the kidneys.

8 medium-sized carrots, trimmed

Handful spinach

$^1/_2$ beet with greens, cut in half

SERVINGS: 2　　　**100% LIVING**

1 Alternately juice the carrots and spinach, tightly bunching up the spinach as you feed it through the machine. Finish by juicing the beet.

2 Pour into individual glasses and serve.

Power-Up Digestive

This is not only good for digestion, but also relieves swelling in the hands and feet.

8 stalks celery

Handful spinach

1 large unwaxed cucumber, quartered

SERVINGS: 2　　　**100% LIVING**

1 Alternately juice 4 of the celery stalks and all of the spinach, tightly bunching up the greens as you feed them through the machine. Then juice the cucumber. Finish by juicing the remaining celery.

2 Pour into individual glasses and serve.

Salad Tonic Digestive

When your meal is composed mostly of cooked foods, this tonic acts as a salad substitute as well as an excellent digestive aid.

1 clove garlic

8 medium-sized carrots, trimmed

$1/_2$ beet with greens, cut in half

1 large tomato, cut up

2 stalks celery

3 medium-sized broccoli florets

2 radishes

SERVINGS: 3   100% LIVING

1 Juice the garlic, followed by the carrots, beet, tomato, celery, broccoli, and radishes.

2 Pour into individual glasses and serve.

Three "C's" Digestive Juice

One of Jay's favorite juice combinations, Three "C's" is so alkaline that hospitals around the world use it to treat ulcers and other acid-related digestive problems.

8 medium-sized carrots, trimmed

2 stalks celery

$1/_4$ head green cabbage, cut into chunks

SERVINGS: 3   100% LIVING

1 Alternately juice 4 of the carrots and all of the celery and cabbage. Finish by juicing the remaining carrots.

2 Pour into individual glasses and serve.

Sweet Popeye

Apples make this combination so yummy that kids will never guess it packs a big nutrient punch.

4 Golden Delicious apples,
  cored and quartered

1/2 cup (38 g) baby spinach

SERVINGS: 1 **100% LIVING**

1 Juice 2 of the apples. Juice the spinach, tightly bunching up the greens as you feed them through the machine. Finish by juicing the remainder of the apples.

2 Pour into a glass and serve.

Bedtime Buddy

The mild sweetness of apples and pears make this a perfect bedtime drink. Remember to choose a firm pear, as very ripe pears don't juice well.

4 Fuji or Red Delicious apples,
  cored and quartered

1 firm pear, cored and
  quartered

SERVINGS: 1 **100% LIVING**

1 Juice first the apples and then the pear.

2 Pour into a glass and serve.

Blue Sky Dreams

Lemon adds a note of tartness to this delightfully blue blend. Use the most deeply colored grapes you can find.

3 Golden Delicious apples, cored and quartered

$1/2$ lemon, rind included

$1/2$ cup (50 g) Ribier grapes or seedless red grapes

SERVINGS: 1   100% LIVING

1 Juice half the apple quarters, followed by the lemon. Juice the grapes, and finish with the remaining apples.

2 Pour into a glass and serve.

Jay's Famous Lemonade

It's hard to tell who enjoys this thirst-quenching favorite more—Jay or the kids. For close to sixty years, Jay has been making this kid- and adult-friendly tonic.

4 Golden Delicious apples, cored and quartered

$1/2$ lemon, rind included

SERVINGS: 1   100% LIVING

1 Juice half the apple quarters. Follow with the lemon, and finish with the remaining apples.

2 Pour into a glass and serve.

Relaxing Charlie

When your kids return home from a hard day of school or sports, Relaxing Charlie will help them unwind while it replaces important vitamins and minerals.

2 Golden Delicious apples, cored and quartered

3 stalks celery

SERVINGS: 1 **100% LIVING**

1 Alternately juice the apples and celery, finishing with a few pieces of apple.

2 Pour into a glass and serve.

Red Parrot

Kids will never guess that the color of this vivid beverage comes from nutrient-rich red beets. We leave out the beet greens because they can make the beverage too bitter for children.

4 Golden Delicious apples, cored and quartered

1/4 beet, without greens

SERVINGS: 2 **100% LIVING**

1 Juice half the apples. Then juice the beet, and follow with the remaining apples.

2 Pour into individual glasses and serve.

Purple Playmate

If your kids love orange juice, this purple twist on an old classic is sure to be a favorite.

1/2 cup (50 g) blueberries

3 Valencia oranges, peeled (with white pith left on) and halved

SERVINGS: 2　　　**100% LIVING**

1 Juice first the blueberries, then the oranges.

2 Pour into individual glasses and serve.

Sunshine Delight

This delicious beverage looks and tastes like pure sunshine.

8 medium-sized carrots, trimmed

2 Golden Delicious apples, cored and quartered.

SERVINGS: 2　　　**100% LIVING**

1 Alternately juice the carrots and apples until all the ingredients have been processed.

2 Pour into individual glasses and serve.

Tropical Medley

Tropical fruit provide the perfect blend of sweet and tart flavors in this golden drink.

1 grapefruit, peeled (with white pith left on) and cut into wedges

1/4 pineapple, peeled and cut into spears

SERVINGS: 1　　　**100% LIVING**

1 Alternately juice the grapefruit and pineapple until all the ingredients have been processed.

2 Pour into a glass and serve.

Left: Liver Mover (see page 181).
Right Back: Jay's Immune Tonic for Life (see page 176).
Right Front: Jay's Sweet Longevity Juice (see page 175).

Jay's Sweet Longevity Juice

If possible, make this juice with Ribier grapes. Because they have not been greatly hybridized, they retain powerful immune-building properties.

1 cup (100 g) Ribier grapes, Concord grapes, or seedless red grapes

$^1/_2$-inch piece fresh ginger, peeled

1 small lemon or lime, rind included, halved

1 Granny Smith apple, cored and quartered

1 cup (144 g) blackberries, raspberries, or blueberries

SERVINGS: 3   100% LIVING

1 Juice the grapes first, followed by the ginger and the lemon or lime. Finish by juicing the apple.

2 Pour the juice into the blender, add the raspberries, and blend until frothy. (Note that if you try to juice the raspberries in the juicer, you will lose some of the fruit in the machine.)

3 Pour into individual glasses and serve.

FOR A CHANGE

◆ To turn this juice into a smoothie, add a banana and $^1/_2$ cup (a few cubes) of ice to the blender, and process until smooth and thick.

Jay's Immune Tonic for Life

Purslane is the key ingredient in this healthful blend, so if it's not readily available in your area, ask your grocer to order it for you. When one of us has a cold or flu, we drink over a quart of this tonic a day to clean the virus out of our system.

Handful purslane

Handful spinach

Handful green or red kale

$^1/_2$ small beet with greens, cut in half

1 clove garlic

$^1/_2$ turnip, cut up

8 medium-sized carrots, trimmed

SERVINGS: 3   100% LIVING

1 First juice the purslane, spinach, and kale, tightly bunching up the greens as you feed them through the machine. Then juice the beet, garlic, and turnip, and finish by juicing the carrots.

2 Pour into individual glasses and serve.

Enzyme-Rich Extravaganza

Enjoy this luscious beverage either on its own or with a fruit salad—never with a vegetable meal. It makes a great breakfast drink and is also an excellent digestive aid because of the powerful enzymes in the papaya.

2 Valencia oranges, peeled (with white pith left on) and halved

2-inch-thick lengthwise slice peeled pineapple

$^1/_2$-inch piece fresh ginger, peeled

2 Golden Delicious apples, cored and quartered

$^1/_2$ small papaya, peeled and seeded

SERVINGS: 3   100% LIVING

1 Juice the orange, pineapple, and ginger. Then juice the apples, and set aside.

2 Place the papaya in a blender, and process until smooth. Add the juice to the blender, and process until well combined.

3 Pour into individual glasses and serve.

Jay's Anti-Aging Tonic

This green drink is the best anti-aging tonic you can make. Remember that when you're green inside, you're clean inside—and healthy!

1/2 cup (38 g) wheatgrass

12 medium-sized carrots, trimmed

1/2 cup (38 g) alfalfa greens

1/2 cup (38 g) dandelion greens

1 cup (75 g) baby spinach

1/2 medium-sized beet with greens, cut in half

3 Granny Smith apples, cored and quartered

SERVINGS: 4   100% LIVING

1 Juice the wheatgrass, tightly bunching it up as you feed it through the machine. Then juice 6 of the carrots, the greens (tightly bunched), the beet, and the apples. Finish by juicing the remaining carrots.

2 Pour into individual glasses and serve.

Wheatgrass for Lightweights

Pure wheatgrass juice is potent stuff and a little hard for some people to get down. This combination—which is a great remedy for stomach ailments—makes wheatgrass more appealing by diluting it with sweet apple juice. Be sure to drink it as soon as you make it; the healing components of wheatgrass don't last long.

2 handfuls wheatgrass

4 apples, any kind, cored and quartered

SERVINGS: 2   100% LIVING

1 Juice half of the wheatgrass followed by 2 of the apples. Repeat until all the ingredients have been juiced, finishing with a few pieces of apple.

2 Pour into individual glasses and serve.

Fresh Mint on the Rocks

The next time you're hot or exhausted, sip this minty summertime beverage and feel instantly refreshed!

Large handful fresh mint

4 Pippin apples, cored and quartered

1 cup ice (about 2 handfuls of cubes)

SERVINGS: 2   100% LIVING

1 Juice the mint first, tightly bunching up the leaves as you feed them through the machine. Then juice the apples.

2 Place the ice in two tall glasses. Pour the juice through a strainer into the individual glasses so that the foam from the apples does not coat the ice. Serve.

FOR A CHANGE

◆ If you really want to cool down, place the juice and ice in a blender, and process until smooth and frosty.

Happy Pancreas Tonic

The combination of Brussels sprouts and string beans helps the pancreas do its job of producing insulin. Carrots and apples lend the combo sweetness.

12 string beans

10 medium-sized carrots, trimmed

4 Brussels sprouts, trimmed

2 Golden Delicious or Pippin apples, cored and quartered

SERVINGS: 3   100% LIVING

1 Juice the string beans first. Juice 5 of the carrots, and follow with the Brussels sprouts and apples. Finish by juicing the remaining carrots.

2 Pour into individual glasses and serve.

Jay's Vital Energy Tonic

We would be lying if we said that this was the best-tasting tonic in our book, but after you drink your first glassful, you'll be so super-energized that you won't care about the flavor. Women should add some raw broccoli for more green power and an extra boost of energy. (See "For a Change.")

8 medium-sized carrots, trimmed

2 inch-piece burdock root

1 clove garlic

1 Jerusalem artichoke, trimmed

Handful spinach

Handful fresh parsley

2 Golden Delicious, Fuji, or Cameo apples, cored and quartered

SERVINGS: 2   100% LIVING

1 Juice 4 of the carrots along with the burdock root and garlic. Then juice the Jerusalem artichoke, followed by the greens, tightly bunching up the leaves as you feed them through the machine. Finish with the apples and the remaining carrots.

2 Pour into individual glasses and serve.

FOR A CHANGE

◆ To make this juice extra-energizing for women, add $1/2$ cup (88 g) broccoli florets before you juice the apples.

Arthur-itis Helper

This fantastic juice combination not only relieves joint pain but also aids digestion. For a milder-tasting beverage that can still help ease the pain, see Pineapple and Apple Juice on page 158.

3-inch-thick lengthwise slice peeled pineapple, cut onto spears

1-inch piece fresh ginger, peeled

SERVINGS: 3   100% LIVING

1 Juice half of the pineapple spears. Follow with the ginger, and finish with the remaining pineapple.

2 Pour into individual glasses and serve.

Cool Cucumber Healing Tonic

In addition to being a great summertime cooler, this tonic acts as a diuretic, eliminating excess fluid and salt from the body.

1 large unwaxed cucumber, quartered

Handful fresh mint

3 large Golden Delicious apples, cored and quartered

SERVINGS: 3   100% LIVING

1 Juice the cucumber. Then juice the mint, tightly bunching up the leaves as you feed them through the machine. Finish by juicing the apples.

2 Pour into individual glasses and serve.

Positively in the Pink

This rosy tonic is the perfect beverage after a workout or time spent in the hot summer sun. It also enhances brain health.

1 pink grapefruit, peeled (with white pith left on) and cut into wedges

2 Red Delicious apples, cored and quartered

1 cup (125 g) raspberries

SERVINGS: 2   100% LIVING

1 Juice first the grapefruit, and then the apples.

2 Pour the juice into the blender, add the raspberries, and blend until frothy. (Note that if you try to juice the raspberries in the juicer, you will lose some of the fruit in the machine.)

3 Pour into individual glasses and serve.

FOR A CHANGE

◆ On an especially hot day, throw 2 cups of ice (a couple of handfuls) into the blender and process until you achieve the desired "slushy" consistency.

Liver Mover

Jay's mentor, Dr. Gerson, introduced this recipe to Jay in 1948. Whether your liver is sluggish or overstimulated, this is a great drink to consume on a daily basis. Serve it with a large vegetable salad.

10 medium-sized carrots, trimmed

1 beet with greens, quartered

2 Golden Delicious apples, cored and quartered

SERVINGS: 3   100% LIVING

1 Alternately juice the carrots, beets, and apples until all the ingredients have been juiced.

2 Pour into individual glasses and serve.

V-12 Super Juice

Like a V-12 engine, this juice can power you through any task. It's also a great accompaniment to Mexican-style foods such as Tofu Tacos (see page 150) and Vegetarian Tacos (see page 149).

Handful spinach

Handful fresh parsley

Handful fresh cilantro

1 large vine-ripened tomato, cut into wedges

$1/2$ red bell pepper

1 clove garlic

8–10 medium-sized carrots, trimmed

SERVINGS: 2   100% LIVING

1 Juice the spinach, parsley, and cilantro, bunching up the greens as you feed them through the machine. Then juice the tomato, red pepper, and garlic. Finish by juicing the carrots.

2 Pour into individual glasses and serve.

Herby Goes Wild

This herbal tonic provides nutrient support for both the liver and the kidneys. Serve it with salads and with any menu that includes cooked foods.

Handful fresh basil

Handful fresh parsley

10 medium-sized carrots, trimmed

2 stalks celery

SERVINGS: 3   100% LIVING

1 Juice the basil and parsley, tightly bunching up the greens as you feed them through the machine. Then alternately juice the carrots and celery, finishing with the carrots.

2 Pour into individual glasses and serve.

Kidney Cleanser

This tart beverage is good for both the kidneys and the bladder. Since fresh cranberries are usually available only during the fall and winter, I suggest freezing a few bags when you can get them so that you're always ready to make this effective tonic.

6 Golden Delicious apples, cored and quartered

15–20 fresh cranberries

SERVINGS: 2   100% LIVING

1 Juice the apples.

2 Pour the apple juice into a blender, and add the cranberries. Process until the cranberries have liquefied.

3 Pour into individual glasses and serve.

FOR A CHANGE

◆ For an icy twist, blend some ice cubes with the cranberry-apple mixture.

Living Nut Milks and Smoothies

Although freshly made vegetable and fruit juices are a staple of a living foods diet, you can enjoy many other beverages while reaping the benefits of live foods. Nut milks are a wonderful choice for people who don't digest milk well, who try to avoid animal products, or who just love the delicious natural taste of these easy-to-make drinks. High in protein and heart-healthy essential fatty acids, nut milks can be served on their own, poured over granola or muesli, or incorporated into blended drinks. Smoothies are another great choice. To make them as wholesome as possible, we recommend using only organic fruits and veggies and purified water. Children love smoothies and also find them fun to make, so you'll want to turn your time in the kitchen into a family activity. These thick, tasty beverages can also be great digestive aids and provide a perfect way to disguise green powder supplements.

Although nut milks can be prepared in a blender and then strained to get a smooth mixture, you can skip this added step if you use the PowerGrind Pro juicer, which pulls out the pulp and quickly produces a wonderfully silky beverage. So plug in your blender or PowerGrind Pro, and get ready to experience delicious nutrient-packed nut milks and smoothies!

> **"Healthy citizens are the greatest asset any country can have."**
> **—Winston Churchill, Statesman**

Living Macadamia Milk

If you love the rich taste of macadamia nuts, you'll want to try our Living Macadamia Milk.

1 cup (125 g) raw whole macadamia nuts

Warm water for soaking

3 cups (711 ml) water

1 teaspoon vanilla extract

1 tablespoon honey, or 2 tablespoons date sugar or coconut sugar

SERVINGS: 4   100% LIVING

1 Place the macadamia nuts in a medium-sized bowl, and add warm water to cover. Allow the nuts to soak at room temperature for at least four hours. If possible, soak overnight.

2 Pour the nuts into a colander, draining and discarding the soaking water. Then rinse with fresh water.

3 Using the PowerGrind Pro's 90-degree shoot, transfer the drained nuts to your juicer and process, adding water to the juicer as it grinds the nuts to produce a nut milk of the desired consistency. Alternatively, place the nuts and water in a blender, and blend on high speed until you have a smooth mixture. Add the vanilla extract and the honey or sugar to the macadamia milk, and process or stir to mix.

4 If you used a blender and you want a pulp-free milk, pour the macadamia milk through a nut milk bag or a cheesecloth-lined strainer, into a bowl or other container. Squeeze the bag or cheesecloth to make sure that all of the milk is extracted. (If desired, you can add the removed pulp to your smoothies.)

5 Use immediately, or place in a covered container and refrigerate for up to two days.

Living Almond Milk

Nutty in flavor, Living Almond Milk can be used in any recipe that calls for milk.

1 cup (150 g) raw whole almonds

Warm water for soaking

4 cups (1 liter) water

SERVINGS: 4　　　　**100% LIVING**

1 Place the almonds in a medium-sized bowl, and add warm water to cover. Allow the nuts to soak overnight at room temperature.

2 Pour the almonds into a colander, draining and discarding the soaking water. Then rinse with fresh water.

3 Using the PowerGrind Pro's 90-degree shoot, transfer the drained almonds to your juicer and process, adding water to the juicer as it grinds the nuts to produce a nut milk of the desired consistency. Alternatively, place the nuts and water in a blender, and blend on high speed until you have a smooth mixture.

4 If you used a blender and you want a pulp-free milk, pour the almond milk through a nut milk bag or a cheesecloth-lined strainer, into a bowl or other container. Squeeze the bag or cheesecloth to make sure that all of the almond milk is extracted. (If desired, you can add the removed pulp to your smoothies.)

5 Use immediately, or place in a covered container and refrigerate for up to two days.

FOR A CHANGE

◆ For Vanilla-Date Living Almond Milk, add 3 pitted dates and 1 tablespoon vanilla extract to the milk, and process in a blender until smooth.

◆ Feel free to replace the almonds in this recipe with a different type of raw nut. Walnuts, pecans, Brazil nuts, hazelnuts, and pistachio nuts will all produce delicious results.

Living Cashew Milk

With a texture like velvet, Living Cashew Milk is a luscious alternative to dairy and soy-based milks.

1 cup (150 g) raw whole cashews

Warm water for soaking

4 cups (1 liter) water

1 teaspoon vanilla extract

SERVINGS: 4   100% LIVING

1 Place the cashews in a medium-sized bowl, and add warm water to cover. Allow the nuts to soak at room temperature for at least four hours. If possible, soak overnight.

2 Pour the cashews into a colander, draining and discarding the soaking water. Then rinse with fresh water.

3 Using the PowerGrind Pro's 90-degree shoot, transfer the drained nuts to your juicer and process, adding water to the juicer as it grinds the nuts to produce a nut milk of the desired consistency. Alternatively, place the nuts and water in a blender, and blend on high speed until you have a smooth mixture. Add the vanilla extract to the cashew milk, and process or stir to mix.

4 If you used a blender and you want a pulp-free milk, pour the cashew milk through a nut milk bag or a cheesecloth-lined strainer, into a bowl or other container. Squeeze the bag or cheesecloth to make sure that all of the milk is extracted. (If desired, you can add the removed pulp to your smoothies.)

5 Use immediately, or place in a covered container and refrigerate for up to two days.

Living Hemp Seed and Pear Milk

Rich, sweet, and milky white, this is a favorite in our home and can be used in any recipe that calls for milk. Because seeds are easier to digest than nuts, hemp milk is easier to digest than nut milk.

2 cups (200 g) raw hemp seeds

Warm water for soaking

4 cups (1 liter) water

1 large or 2 small firm pears, cored and quartered

SERVINGS: 4   100% LIVING

1 Place the hemp seeds in a medium-sized bowl, and add warm water to cover. Allow the seeds to soak overnight at room temperature.

2 Pour the seeds into a fine-mesh colander (so that the seeds don't slip through), draining and discarding the soaking water. Then rinse with fresh water.

3 Using the PowerGrind Pro's 90-degree shoot, transfer the drained hemp seeds to the juicer and process, adding water to the juicer as it grinds the nuts. Finish off with the pear. Alternatively, place the seeds, water, and pear in a blender, and blend on high speed until you have a smooth mixture.

4 If you used a blender and you want a pulp-free milk, pour the milk through a nut milk bag or a cheesecloth-lined strainer, into a bowl or other container. Squeeze the bag or cheesecloth to make sure that all of the seed milk is extracted. (If desired, you can add the removed pulp to your smoothies.)

5 Use immediately, or place in a covered container and refrigerate for up to two days.

Living Sesame and Macadamia Nut Milk

A combination of sesame seeds and macadamia nuts give this milk a unique, ultra-rich flavor.

1 cup (115 g) raw sesame seeds

$^1/_2$ cup (62 g) raw whole macadamia nuts

Warm water for soaking

3 cups (711 ml) water

2 Golden Delicious apples, cored and quartered

SERVINGS: 4   100% LIVING

1 Place the sesame seeds and macadamia nuts in a medium-sized bowl, and add warm water to cover. Allow the nuts and seeds to soak for four hours at room temperature.

2 Pour the seeds and nuts into a fine-mesh colander (so that the seeds don't slip through), draining and discarding the soaking water. Then rinse with fresh water.

3 Using the PowerGrind Pro's 90-degree shoot, transfer the drained seeds and nuts to your juicer and process, adding water to the juicer as it grinds the nuts. Finish off with the apples. Alternatively, place the seeds and nuts, water, and apples in a blender, and blend on high speed until you have a smooth mixture.

4 If you used a blender and you want a pulp-free milk, pour the milk through a nut milk bag or a cheesecloth-lined strainer, into a bowl or other container. Squeeze the bag or cheesecloth to make sure that all of the milk is extracted. (If desired, you can add the removed pulp to your smoothies.)

5 Use immediately, or place in a covered container and refrigerate for up to two days.

Living Tropical Nut Milk

Sweet and creamy, with a lovely light pink color, this tropical milk makes a wonderful beverage or a great topping for granola. The flax seeds give the milk body and also aid digestion.

1 cup (150 g) raw whole cashews

Warm water for soaking

$^1/_2$ cup (90 g) raw flax seeds

Warm water for soaking

1 large papaya, peeled, seeded, and cut into chunks

$^1/_2$ cup (118 ml) water

SERVINGS: 4   100% LIVING

1 Place the cashews in a medium-sized bowl, and add warm water to cover. Allow the nuts to soak overnight at room temperature

2 Several hours before youe make the milk, place the flax seeds in a medium-sized bowl, and add warm water to cover. Allow the seeds to soak for at least four hours at room temperature.

3 Pour the cashews into a colander, draining and discarding the soaking water. Then rinse with fresh water. Do *not* drain the flax seeds.

4 Using the PowerGrind Pro's 90-degree shoot, transfer the undrained flax seeds to the juicer, and begin juicing. Follow with half of the papaya followed by half the cashews, the rest of the papaya, and the remainder of the cashews. Then add the water. Alternatively, place all of the ingredients in a blender, and blend on low speed for about a minute, or until the mixture is smooth and frothy.

5 If you used a blender and you want a pulp-free milk, pour the milk through a nut milk bag or a cheesecloth-lined strainer, into a bowl or other container. Squeeze the bag or cheesecloth to make sure that all of the milk is extracted. (If desired, you can add the removed pulp to your smoothies.)

6 Use immediately, or place in a covered container and refrigerate for up to two days.

High-Protein Nut Smoothie

If you have time, start soaking the nuts and seeds the night before you prepare this protein-packed smoothie. If not, a two-hour soaking will do.

2 tablespoons walnuts

2 tablespoons almonds

2 tablespoons sunflower seeds

2 tablespoons flax seeds

Warm water for soaking

4 cups (1 liter) water

1 cup (100 g) fresh or frozen blueberries, or the berries of your choice

2 medium bananas, cut into chunks

2 tablespoons honey or coconut sugar

SERVINGS: 3   100% LIVING

1 Place the nuts and seeds in a medium-sized bowl, and pour the warm water over them. Allow to sit for at least four hours, or preferably, overnight.

2 Pour the soaked nuts and seeds into a sieve, and discard the soaking water. Then rinse with fresh water.

3 Place the drained nuts and seeds and all the remaining ingredients in a blender, and blend on high speed until smooth.

4 Pour into individual glasses and serve.

Date a Banana
for Breakfast Smoothie

This filling smoothie makes a perfect breakfast when you're facing a busy day. Creamy and delicious, it will keep you satisfied for hours.

$^3/_4$ cup (94 g) chopped walnuts

Warm water for soaking

1 $^1/_2$ cups (355 ml) Living Almond Milk (see page 186)

2 bananas, cut into chunks

$^1/_2$ cup (113 g) pitted dates

SERVINGS: 4   100% LIVING

1 Place the walnuts in a medium-sized bowl, and add warm water to cover. Allow to sit for at least four hours, or preferably, overnight.

2 Pour the soaked nuts into a sieve, and discard the soaking water.

3 Place the drained nuts and all of the remaining ingredients in a blender, and process until the mixture is smooth.

4 Pour into individual glasses and serve.

FOR A CHANGE

◆ Enhance the flavor of this smoothie by blending in $^1/_2$ teaspoon of pure vanilla extract.

◆ For a different taste and consistency, replace the walnuts with $^1/_2$ cup (56 g) chopped almonds, which have been soaked and drained. Place the drained almonds, the remaining ingredients, $^1/_2$ cup (118 ml) water, and 1 cup (a handful or two) of ice in the blender. Blend until smooth.

Our Morning
Digestion Perfection Smoothie

This luscious tropical blend is a great way to start the morning. It's also an effective way to heal the inner lining of the stomach when too much caffeine, alcohol, or white sugar has created digestive disturbances.

1 baby coconut and its liquid*

1 orange, peeled and cut into pieces

1-inch piece fresh ginger, peeled

$^1/_2$ cup (118 ml) fresh lemon juice

Pinch cayenne pepper

* See page 91 for preparation instructions.

SERVINGS: 2   100% LIVING

1 Place all of the ingredients in a blender, and process until smooth.

2 Pour into individual glasses and serve.

FOR A CHANGE

◆ If you find even this drink difficult to digest, add 1 tablespoon of powdered enzymes and 1 tablespoon of powdered or liquid acidophilus to the blender right before serving.

Good Morning Power-Up Smoothie (see page 195).

Good Morning Power-Up Smoothie

This is Linda's favorite supergreen drink, and it's a wonderful way to supplement the greens in your diet. To maximize the benefits of this smoothie, make sure that the green powder and other supplements are free of sugar and other additives.

---

3 cups water

3 bananas, cut into pieces

$^1/_2$ cup (50 g) fresh or frozen blueberries

$^1/_3$ cup green powder supplement

1 tablespoon spirulina

1 tablespoon bee pollen

1 tablespoon powdered vitamin C

1 tablespoon liquid chlorophyll

1 tablespoon powdered enzymes

2 teaspoons powdered or liquid acidophilus

SERVINGS: 4   100% LIVING

1 Place all of the ingredients in a blender, and process until smooth.

2 Pour into individual glasses and serve.

The Date from Heaven Smoothie

Baby coconuts contain substances that help heal the lining of the stomach, making this a great beverage for anyone with ulcers or other digestive problems. Ginger, a well-known digestive aid, doubles this smoothie's healing power.

2 baby coconuts and their liquid*

2 bananas, cut into chunks

6 pitted dates

$^1/_3$ cup (42 g) macadamia nuts

$^1/_3$ pineapple, peeled and cut into chunks

$^1/_2$-inch piece fresh ginger, peeled

2 cups ice (several handfuls)

* See page 91 for preparation instructions.

SERVINGS: 3   100% LIVING

1 Place all of the ingredients except for the ice in a blender, and blend for several minutes, or until all of the ingredients have been liquefied. Add the ice, and continue to blend until the mixture has the desired consistency.

2 Pour into individual glasses and serve.

"It's bizarre that the produce manager is more important to my children's health than the pediatrician."
—Meryl Streep, Actress

Very Berry Powerful Smoothie (see page 198).

Very Berry Powerful Smoothie

Berries are packed with powerful blood detoxifiers and brain stimulators, turning this into a wonderful tonic as well as a super-delicious smoothie. If you can't get fresh berries, purchase frozen organic produce, use what you need, and keep the rest in the freezer for your next smoothie-making adventure.

4 Red Delicious or Golden Delicious apples, cored and quartered

2 oranges, peeled (with white pith left on) and cut into wedges

$1/2$ lime with skin

8 blueberries

6 blackberries

6 raspberries

6 strawberries

1 large banana, cut into chunks

1 cup ice (about 2 handfuls)

SERVINGS: 4   100% LIVING

1 Juice the apples, oranges, and lime.

2 Place the juices in a blender, add the berries and banana, and blend until smooth. Add the ice, and blend until the mixture has the desired consistency.

3 Pour into individual glasses and serve.

Young Coconut Dream

Dr. Rob Young and his beautiful wife, Shelley, shared this recipe with us, and now we want to share it with you! It is both a refreshing smoothie and an amazing alkalizing tonic.

1 large unwaxed cucumber, quartered

1 lime, rind included, halved

3 kale leaves

1 large handful spinach

1 large handful fresh parsley

1 medium zucchini, quartered

1 Golden Delicious apple, cored and quartered

1 large avocado (preferably Haas), peeled and cut into chunks

1 baby coconut and its liquid*

* See page 91 for preparation instructions.

SERVINGS: 4   100% LIVING

1 Juice the cucumber first, followed by the lime. Then juice the greens, tightly bunching them up as you feed them through the machine. Juice the zucchini, and finish by juicing the apple.

2 Transfer the juice to a blender, and add the avocado and the meat and water of the baby coconut. Blend until smooth.

3 Pour into individual glasses and serve.

"No disease that can be treated by diet should be treated with any other means."

—Maimonides, Philosopher and Physician

Carob Smoothie

This high-protein, low-fat smoothie is perfect for breakfast. Carob and molasses add chocolatey flavor and color, and the nut and seed "crunchies" make this beverage simply irresistible. I sometimes call it my Muesli Smoothie!

2 cups (474 ml) Living Almond Milk (see page 186)

3 bananas, cut into chunks and frozen

$^1/_2$ cup (80 g) frozen acai berries

$^1/_4$ cup (81 g) blackstrap molasses

3 $^1/_2$ tablespoons carob powder

$^1/_2$ teaspoon ground cinnamon (for garnish)

1 teaspoon sunflower seeds (for garnish)

1 teaspoon hemp seeds (for garnish)

6 pecans, chopped (for garnish)

SERVINGS: 4   **100% LIVING**

1 Place all of the ingredients except for the garnishes in a blender. Process until the mixture is smooth.

2 Pour into individual glasses, and garnish each serving with cinnamon, sunflower seeds, hemp seeds, and pecans. Serve.

FOR A CHANGE

◆ Instead of using the seeds and nuts, garnish each smoothie with a liberal sprinkling of Loving Living Granola (see page 127).

Pâtés, Dips, and Spreads

Nutritious, delicious, and a snap to prepare, the dips and spreads in this section are incredibly versatile. They can elevate just about any living or cooked dish—salads, sandwiches, breads, or crackers—to delectable new heights.

Living Cucumber Nut Pâté

Spread this luscious pâté on flax seed crackers or breads, or use it as a filling for cucumber boats, zucchini boats, or celery stalks.

1 cucumber, peeled and cut into chunks

1 cup (144 g) sunflower seeds, soaked overnight and drained

¼ medium-sized yellow onion

1 clove garlic, crushed

Water for desired consistency

Sea salt and black pepper to taste

YIELD: 2–2½ CUPS   100% LIVING

1 Place the cucumber, drained sunflower seeds, onion, and garlic in a food processor or wide-mouth blender, and process on low speed for about one minute, or until the mixture has the desired consistency. If it is too thick, add water, a little at a time, until it is spreadable but not runny. Season to taste with salt and pepper.

2 Transfer the mixture to a serving bowl and enjoy immediately, or place in an airtight container and refrigerate for up to two days.

FOR A CHANGE

◆ For a spicy kick, substitute 2 teaspoons Cajun seasoning for the salt and pepper.

Homemade Hummus

Everyone loves this delicious Middle Eastern classic! Add a spoonful to just about any salad, enjoy it as a sandwich spread, or serve it as a dip with raw vegetables.

1 cup (224 g) cooked garbanzo beans

8 ounces (252 g) firm tofu*

3 large cloves garlic

$\frac{1}{4}$ cup (7 g) chopped fresh parsley

$\frac{1}{4}$ cup (59 ml) fresh lemon juice

1 tablespoon paprika

2 teaspoons tahini

2 teaspoons sea salt

1 teaspoon black pepper

*An especially healthy choice is non-GMO organic sprouted tofu.

YIELD: ABOUT 2 CUPS   20% LIVING

1 Place all of the ingredients in a food processor or wide-mouth blender, and process until smooth and creamy.

2 Transfer the mixture to a serving bowl and sprinkle with a little paprika. Enjoy immediately, or place in an airtight container and refrigerate for up to five days.

FOR A CHANGE

◆ Instead of parsley, use chopped fresh cilantro.

◆ Before serving, top with a sprinkling of finely chopped cilantro (or parsley) or a drizzle of olive oil.

◆ For a burst of heat, use chili powder instead of paprika.

Super-Simple Guacamole

Be sure to try this easy-to-prepare classic dip with our Whole World Tostadas (see page 151).

4 ripe avocados (preferably Haas), peeled and pitted

2–3 tablespoons finely chopped yellow onion

3 tablespoons fresh lime juice

Sea salt to taste

YIELD: ABOUT 4 CUPS   100% LIVING

1 Place the avocados in a mixing bowl, and coarsely mash with a fork.

2 Add the remaining ingredients and stir until well blended.

3 Serve immediately, or place in an airtight container and store in the refrigerator for one day.

FOR A CHANGE

◆ Toss in a handful of chopped fresh cilantro for added flavor.

Eggless Tofu Mayonnaise

This mayonnaise makes a rich and flavorful sandwich spread. You can also stir a spoonful or two into most salad dressings for added creaminess.

15 ounces (420 g) firm tofu*

1 ½ tablespoons fresh lemon juice

1 teaspoon date sugar or coconut sugar

1 teaspoon sea salt

½ teaspoon dry mustard

⅛ teaspoon white pepper

*An especially healthy choice is non-GMO organic sprouted tofu.

YIELD: ABOUT 2 CUPS   20% LIVING

1 Place all of the ingredients in a food processor or wide-mouth blender, and process until smooth and creamy.

2 Use immediately, or place in an airtight container and refrigerate for up to two weeks.

Our Favorite Simple Salsa

In addition to adding some of this fresh vibrant salsa to our living soups and basic cooked salads, be sure to spoon some over our Whole World Tostadas (see page 151) and Tofu Tacos (see page 150).

3 cups (600 g) diced vine-ripened roma or plum tomatoes

$^1/_2$ cup (13 g) chopped fresh cilantro

$^1/_2$ cup (13 g) minced fresh parsley

$^1/_4$ cup (38 g) diced yellow onion

1 clove garlic, crushed

Juice of 2 limes or lemons

2 teaspoons minced jalapeño pepper

$^1/_2$ teaspoon sea salt

YIELD: ABOUT 3 $^1/_2$ CUPS   100% LIVING

1 Place all of the ingredients in a mixing bowl, and stir well.

2 Serve immediately or refrigerate and enjoy chilled. Store leftovers in an airtight container and refrigerate for up to three days.

FOR A CHANGE

◆ For increased visual appeal, include diced yellow and/or orange heirloom tomatoes (when in season) in this salsa.

Living Celery Nut Spread

Delicious on sandwiches and as a topper for salads, this appetizing spread is always a hit! Make sure the almonds are soaked overnight for easier blending and to keep the spread from becoming dry.

5 stalks celery, cut into chunks

1 cup (150 g) almonds, soaked overnight and drained

1 avocado (preferably Haas), peeled and pitted

3 tablespoons chopped yellow onion

3 tablespoons chopped fresh parsley

Juice of 1 medium lemon

2 tablespoons tamari or Bragg Liquid Aminos

1 tablespoon Bernard Jensen's Vegetable Seasoning or Spike seasoning

$\frac{1}{2}$ teaspoon ground sage

$\frac{1}{4}$ teaspoon paprika

YIELD: 2–2 $\frac{1}{2}$ CUPS   100% LIVING

1 Place all of the ingredients in a food processor or wide-mouth blender, and process on low speed until the mixture is smooth and thick.

2 Transfer the mixture to a serving bowl and enjoy immediately, or place in an airtight container and refrigerate for up to two days.

FOR A CHANGE

◆ If you have to avoid gluten, be sure to buy a gluten-free brand of tamari or to use Bragg Liquid Aminos, which is gluten-free.

◆ Instead of serving this spread in a bowl, shape it into a loaf and serve on a platter, surrounded by leafy greens, chopped tomatoes, and chopped onions.

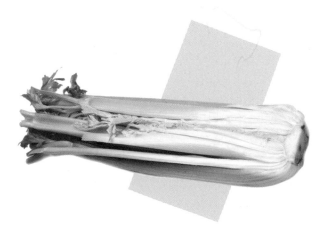

Our Resources

As you start your transition to a better diet and a healthier lifestyle, you will need all the support you can get while steering clear of bad information and poor products. Throughout the years—during the course of each day of healthy living, and also while teaching seminars on juicing and living foods—we have accumulated a list of reliable resources, including informational websites, producers of organic foods, suppliers of organic gardening supplies, and much more. The listings below were created to share our resources with you. As you will see, to make it as easy as possible for you to locate what you're looking for, we have broken the listings into the following six categories: Home Gardening and Sprouting; Live Food Programs and Alternate Healing; Medicinal Healing with Herbs and Flower Essences; Nutritional Supplements; Organic Foods and Self-Care Products; and Vegetarian and Vegan Diet Support. Each listing includes contact information—whenever possible, a full address, telephone number, and web address. (Sometimes, only a website or a website and phone number are available.) If you are interested in furthering your knowledge through books, you'll find a list of Recommended Readings on page 215.

HOME GARDENING AND SPROUTING

Seeds of Change
PO Box 4908
Rancho Dominguez, CA 90220
Phone: 888-762-7333
Website: www.seedsofchange.com

This company offers only certified organic, open-pollinated seeds for people who want to grow their own organic vegetables, herbs, and other produce. Tools and other gardening supplies are also available.

Sprout People
Website: www.sproutpeople.org

Sprout People offers an extensive selection of certified organic seeds, sprouts, and sprouting supplies—including convenient kits and seed samplers—for home use.

LIVE FOOD PROGRAMS AND ALTERNATIVE HEALING

The Ann Wigmore Foundation (AWF)
PO Box 398
San Fidel, NM 87049
Phone: 505-552-0595
Website: www.wigmore.org

Based on the teachings of Anne Wigmore, the AWF—formerly known as the Hippocrates Health Institute—offers ten-day retreats for the purpose of teaching the Living Foods Lifestyle.

Burzynski Clinic
9432 Katy Freeway
Houston, TX 77055
Phone: 800-714-7181
Website: www.burzynskiclinic.com

This world-famous clinic offers customized cancer treatment regimens based on the natural biochemical defense system of the body.

Gerson Institute
PO Box 161358
San Diego, CA 92176
Phone: 888-443-7766
Website: www.gerson.org

A nonprofit organization founded by Charlotte Gerson—the daughter of Dr. Max Gerson, who cured Jay Kordich with the original raw juice therapy program—this is a live-in alternative treatment center and cancer clinic.

Jay and Linda Kordich's School of Juicing
Website: www.schoolofjuicing.com

Jay and Linda Kordich offer a comprehensive multimedia program designed to guide you in regaining your health through juicing.

Oasis of Hope Hospital
Paseo Playas #19, Seccion Monumental
Playas de Tijuana
Tijuana, Baja California, Mexico 22504
Phone: 888-500-4673
Website: www.oasisofhope.com

Founded by Dr. Ernesto Contreras, Sr., Oasis of Hope provides individualized cancer treatments that combine the latest conventional therapies with alternative approaches, emotional support, and spiritual counseling.

Optimum Health Institute (OHI)
6970 Central Avenue
Lemon Grove, CA 91945
Phone: 800-993-4325
Website: www.optimumhealth.org

With centers in southern California and central Texas, the OHI provides a wholistic healing program that emphasizes mental, emotional, spiritual, and physical health. Internal body cleansing and detoxification form the cornerstone of the center's physical health program.

pH Miracle Living
16390 Dia Del Sol
Valley Center, CA 92082
Phone: 760-751-8321
Website: www.phmiracleliving.com

Dr. Robert Young and Shelley Young offer coaching, retreats, a group cleanse program, and a range of supplements and other products that support an alkaline diet and lifestyle.

Tree of Life Rejuvenation Center
PO Box 778
Patagonia, AZ 85624
Phone: 866-394-2520
Website: www.gabrielcousens.com

Founded by Dr. Gabriel Cousens, this center is a plant-source-only live food, residential guest, and student center that promotes spiritual growth and whole-body health.

MEDICINAL HEALING WITH HERBS AND FLOWER ESSENCES

American Botanical Council
PO Box 144345
Austin, TX 78714
Phone: 800-373-7105
Website: www.herbalgram.org

This nonprofit research and education organization is dedicated to providing accurate information on the use of herbs and medicinal plants. HerbalGram, its scientific quarterly journal, is available for a fee.

American Herbalists Guild
PO Box 230741
Boston, MA 02123
Phone: 617-520-4372
Website: www.americanherbalistsguild.com

Designed to establish a standard of competency among practitioners of botanical medicine, this guild offers an easy-to-use "Find an Herbalist" feature on its website.

Blessed Herbs
Phone: 800-489-4372
Website: www.blessedherbs.com

This company offers all-natural cleansing and detoxification kits, as well as bulk herbs and liquid extracts.

The Flower Essence Society
Phone: 800-736-9222
Website: www.flowersociety.org

Through its website, the Flower Essence Society provides articles on the therapeutic use of flower-based remedies.

Herb Pharm
PO Box 116
Williams, OR 97544
Phone: 800-348-4372
Website: www.herb-pharm.com

Herb Pharm offers a full line of organic herbal extracts for medicinal use.

Herb Research Foundation
Website: www.herbs.org

Through its website, this foundation provides solid scientific information about herbs.

NUTRITIONAL SUPPLEMENTS

Arise & Shine
Phone: 800-688-2444
Website: www.ariseandshine.com

This company specializes in herbal formulas designed to cleanse and detoxify the body. Also available are probiotics, alkalizers, and other supplements, as well as educational materials on cleansing.

Barlean's Organic Oils
3660 Slater Road
Ferndale, WA 98248
Phone: 800-445-3529
Website: www.barleans.com
Barlean's produces pure, certified organic flax seed oil, flax oil blends, fish oils, specialty oils, and green superfood supplements.

Jay Kordich
221 First Avenue West, Suite 350
Seattle, WA 98119
Phone: 800-279-2507
Website: www.jaykordich.com

Jay Kordich offers his newest juicer; books and audio products; natural supplements such as enzymes, probiotics, and green powders; and an all-natural produce cleaner.

Omega Nutrition
1695 Franklin Street
Vancouver, BC V5L 1P5
Phone: 800-661-3529
Website: www.omeganutrition.com

Specializing in flax seed oil, this company also offers coconut and pumpkin seed oils.

ORGANIC FOODS AND SELF-CARE PRODUCTS

Bates Nut Farm
15954 Woods Valley Road
Valley Center, CA 92082
Phone: 760-749-3333
Website: www.batesnutfarm.biz

Bates offers a variety of nuts and dried fruits, including healthful raw nuts.

Cherry Moon Farms
Phone: 800-580-2913
Website: www.cherrymoonfarms.com

Cherry Moon carries both organic and nonorganic food gifts.

Dr. Bronner's Magic Soaps
PO Box 28
Escondido, CA 92033
Phone: 877-786-3649
Website: www.drbronner.com

This company offers organic all-natural products, including virgin coconut oil (for cooking and personal use) and a range of soaps, lotions, and other personal-care items.

Exotic Superfoods
Phone: 917-685-2586 (Queens, NY)
          347-804-3961 (Los Angeles, CA)

Exotic Superfoods sells raw organic packaged coconut meat and coconut water.

Fiddler's Green Farm
PO Box 254
Belfast, ME 04915
Phone: 800-729-7935
Website: www.fiddlersgreenfarm.com

This certified organic family farm sells freshly stone-ground flours, dried beans, and many other healthful products.

Frog Hollow Farm
PO Box 2110
Brentwood, CA 94513
Phone: 888-779-4511
Website: www.froghollow.com

An organic farm, Frog Hollow ships out fresh seasonal fruit, dried fruit, and other products.

Frontier Cooperative Herbs
PO Box 299
3021 78th Street
Norway, IA 52318
Phone: 800-669-3275
Website: www.frontiercoop.com

This company sells organic herbs, spices, teas, and other foods.

Gourmet Greens
198 Dodge Road
Chester, VT 05143
Phone: 866-808-7392
Website: www.gourmetgreens.com

Gourmet Greens produces and sells certified organic wheatgrass and greens, wheatgrass seeds, and wheatgrass juicers.

Local Harvest
Website: www.localharvest.org

This helpful website enables you to locate farmer's markets, family farms, and other sources of sustainably grown foods in your area. Click on the "Shop" tab to find organic farms—such as Beck Grove and Blue Heron Botanicals—that can ship organic produce.

McFadden Farm
16000 Powerhouse Road
Potter Valley, CA 95469
Phone: 800-544-8230
Website: www.mcfaddenfarm.com

McFadden Farm offers organic herbs and herb blends.

Mendocino Sea Vegetable Company
PO Box 455
Philo, CA 95466
Phone: 707-895-2996
Website: www.seaweed.net

This company offers wild-crafted dried North American kombu, dulse, and other sea vegetables.

Noni Fruit Leather
Website: www.real-noni.com

This company sells organic noni fruit leather and other noni products.

Nuts.com
125 Moen Street
Cranford, NJ 07016
Phone: 800-558-6887
Website: www.nuts.com

Nuts.com offers a range of certified organic nuts, seeds, and dried fruits, including raw nuts.

Ozark Forest Mushrooms
Phone: 314-531-9935
Website: www.ozarkforest.com

Ozark offers wild mushrooms and mushroom-growing kits for home use.

Salt Works, Inc.
16240 Wood-Red Road, NE
Woodinville, WA 98072
Phone: 800-353-7258
Website: www.saltworks.us

Salt Works offers premium gourmet sea salts and bath salts.

South Tex Organics, LC
PO Box 808
Mission, TX 78573
Phone: 888-895-0108
Website: www.stxorganics.com

These organic growers specialize in grapefruit, oranges, and lemons.

Spring Tree Corporation
Phone: 516-333-9326
Website: sbamerica.com

Based in Vermont, Spring Tree produces pure maple syrup.

Sun Organic Farms
Phone: 888-269-9888
Website: www.sunorganicfarm.com

Sun Organic offers a wide range of organic foods and products, including beans, grains, nuts, oils, pastas, and much more.

Thistle Dew Farm
RR1 Box 122
Proctor, WV 26055
Phone: 800-854-6639
Website: www.thistledewfarm.com

Thistle Dew sells gifts from the honeybee, including honeycomb, honey, beeswax, skin cream, and candles.

Tierra Farm
2424 State Route 203
Valatie, NY 12184
Phone: 888-674-6887
Website: www.tierrafarm.com

This certified organic New York farm offers a variety of premium raw nuts and seeds sourced mostly from domestic growers.

Wood Prairie Farm
49 Kinney Road
Bridgewater, ME 04735
Phone: 800-829-9765
Website: www.woodprairie.com

This certified organic Maine farm sells specialty potatoes, grains and flours, dried beans, organic seeds and growing supplies, and a range of other great products.

VEGETARIAN AND VEGAN DIET SUPPORT

American Vegan Society (AVS)
56 Dinshah Lane
PO Box 369
Malaga, NJ 08328
Website: www.americanvegan.org

A nonprofit educational organization, the AVS was created to explore, promote, and support a compassionate vegan diet and lifestyle.

EarthSave
20555 Devonshire Street, Suite 105
Chatsworth, CA 91311
Website: www.earthsave.org

A nonprofit organization, EarthSave, through its website, offers a wealth of information on healthy eating.

Recommended Readings

The following books offer more information about vegetarian living, raw foods, juicing, food enzymes, and other topics of interest. These titles—as well as other books by the authors listed below—can provide not only important information but also the support you need as you improve both your diet and your lifestyle.

Cousens, Gabriel. *Conscious Eating.* **North Atlantic Books, 2000.**
Called the "Bible of Vegetarians," *Conscious Eating* offers information on live food cuisine, enzymes, and other topics of interest.

Gerson, Max. *A Cancer Therapy: Results of Fifty Cases and the Cure of Advanced Cancer by Diet Therapy.* **Gerson Institute, 1958.**
This is Dr. Gerson's most complete book on the use of his diet therapy to reactivate the body's healing mechanisms and cure cancer.

Kloss, Jethro. *Back to Eden.* **Back to Eden Publishing, 2004.**
Now updated and expanded, this is a classic text on herbs, natural diet and lifestyle, and wholistic health.

Kordich, Jay. *The Juiceman's Power of Juicing.* **Grand Central Publishing, 1993.**
This introduction to the health benefits of juicing includes nearly a hundred recipes for fruit and vegetable juices.

Murray, Michael T. *The Complete Book of Juicing.* **Clarkson Potter, 1997.**
The author presents information on the healing power of juices along with over 150 juice recipes.

Santillo, Humbart. *Food Enzymes: The Missing Link to Radiant Health.* **Lotus Press, 1993.**
Written for both the lay person and the health practitioner, this book—an excellent introduction to the food enzyme concept—includes issues such as digestive health and weight control.

Young, Robert, and Young, Shelley. *The pH Miracle: Balance Your Diet, Reclaim Your Health.* **Grand Central Life & Style, 2010.**
In this book, the Youngs offer a program for cleansing the body and balancing its pH for optimum health.

Index

effect of, on enzymes, 37–38

effect of, on fiber, 38

Cookware and appliances, assessing, for the living kitchen, 66–67

Cool Cucumber Healing Tonic, 180

Cool-Weather Fruit Salad, Basic, 92

Cousens, Gabriel, 11, 13

Cucumber Nut Pâté, Living, 201

D

Dairy products, avoidance of, 69

Date a Banana for Breakfast Smoothie, 192

Date from Heaven Smoothie, The, 196

Dehydrator, 67

oven as alternative to, 128

Deli meats, avoidance of, 69

Diabetes

choosing fruits for juicing, 20

limiting carrots in juice combinations for, 18

Digestion

Jay's tips for better, 43

role of enzymes in, 35, 36, 37, 38–39

Digestive Calming Tonic, 165

Digestive Companion, 165

Digestive enzymes, 37. *See also* Enzymes.

Digestive Juice Aid recipes

Basic Digestive Tonic, 164

Blood-Building Digestive, 164

Digestive Calming Tonic, 165

Digestive Companion, 165

Green Power Tummy Remedy, 166

Green Tummy Machine, 167

Heavy-Duty Green Digestive, 166

Meal Sipper Digestive, 167

Popeye's Digestive Special, 168

Power-Up Digestive, 168

Salad Tonic Digestive, 169

Three "C's" Digestive Juice, 169

See also Digestion, Jay's tips for better; Juice recipes.

Dips. *See* Pâtés, Dips, and Spreads.

Dressings, salad. *See* Salad dressing recipes.

Dried fruits. *See* Fruits, dried.

E

Eating habits, changing

emotional benefits of, 50

handling lapses during, 50–51

ninety-day program for, 30–32

physical benefits of, 50–51

Egg Salad, Better Than, 106

Eggless Tofu Mayonnaise, 204

Emotional benefits of living foods diet, 50

Enzyme supplements, 40

Enzyme-Rich Extravaganza, 176

Enzymes

"bank account" of, in body, 37–38

ensuring benefits of, 40–44

ensuring diet rich in, 39–40

maintaining power of, in juice, 13

role of, in body, 35–36

role of, in digestion, 35, 36, 37, 38–9

source of, in juice, 13

supplements of, 40

F

Fasting, juice. *See* Juice fast.

Flavorings, recommended, 72

Food enzymes, 37. *See also* Enzymes.

Food Pyramids. *See* Green Salad Pyramid; Natural Food Pyramid.

Foods

to be eliminated from living kitchen, 69–70

buying, washing, and storing of, 75–79

recommended for living foods diet, 70–74

Fresh Gazpacho, 130

Fresh Herb Salad Dressing, 118

Fresh Mint on the Rocks, 178

The Jay Kordich PowerGrind Pro Longevity Juicer

Features

- Revolutionary new slow juicer hybrid technology.
- Four international patents.
- Delivers more juice and nutrients than other juicers.
- Makes both soy and almond milk.
- Super quiet induction motor.
- 1 year manufacturer's warranty.
- Heavy duty surgical quality stainless steel blade.
- Patented double feed chute.
- Extra-large detachable pulp basket.
- Powerful motor never bogs down.
- Low RPM preserves juice quality.
- Easy to clean. Parts are dishwasher safe.
- Perfect for making leafy green juices.
- Operations guide DVD featuring Jay.

Jay's Powergrind Pro Longevity juicer has revolutionized the juicing industry. Its patented new technology delivers more juice and nutrients per ounce of produce, stretching your food dollar. It uses hybrid technology combining both extracting and grinding to deliver the best quality in juice. This not only yields more juice but also helps preserve more nutrients and enzymes.

The Powergrind Pro Longevity juicer is easy to use, easy to clean and enables you to make a wider variety of juices than other juicers on the market. It is perfect for fruits and vegetables, leafy greens AND makes almond and other nut milks. The Powergrind Pro Longevity juicer truly provides the best value available today.

Visit **www.JayKordich.com**
and use Promo Code: POWERGRIND10
to save 10% on Jay's PowerGrind Longevity Juicer. It is available exclusively at
www.JayKordich.com.

The Jay Kordich PowerGrind Pro Vitality Juicer

Features

- Multi-Patented slow juicer hybrid technology.
- Both extracts & grinds.
- Easily makes nut milks in one simple step.
- More efficient with leafy green vegetables than most juicers.
- Produces up to 30% more juice per ounce of produce.
- Produces superior juice quality, taste, texture and color.
- Unique double feed tube for juicing mixologists.
- Low 3600 RPM, "slow juicing preserves more nutrients and enzymes"
- Easy to clean, dishwasher safe, PBA free.

The new PowerGrind Vitality Juicer shares the same features and quality construction as its big brother, the PowerGrind Pro Longevity. To assemble, disassemble and to clean is extremely easy making it very simple to use. There is no need for any special preparation of fruits and vegetables. This is a great juicer for a single person or someone just getting started juicing.

The PowerGrind Vitality juicer also uses a patented hybrid/slow juicing technology. Its two step process allows it to both grind AND extract juice more efficiently. This gives you up to 30% more juice from the same amount of produce as other juicers, helping to stretch your food dollar. It will prepare ALL kinds of juices; works extremely well with leafy green vegetables, and the PROS are the only juicers that make nut milks. Its compact size takes up less space in your kitchen, also making it perfect for travel.

Visit **www.JayKordich.com**
and use Promo Code: POWERGRIND10
to save 10% on Jay's PowerGrind Vitality Juicer. It is available exclusively at
www.JayKordich.com.

THE ACID-ALKALINE FOOD GUIDE
A Quick Reference to Foods & Their Effect on pH Levels
Dr. Susan E. Brown and Larry Trivieri, Jr.

In the last few years, researchers around the world have reported the importance of acid-alkaline balance to good health. While thousands of people are trying to balance their body's pH level, until now, they have had to rely on guides containing only a small number of foods. *The Acid-Alkaline Food Guide* is a complete resource for people who want to widen their food choices.

The book begins by explaining how the acid-alkaline environment of the body is influenced by foods. It then presents a list of thousands of foods—single foods, combination foods, and even fast foods—and their acid-alkaline effects. *The Acid-Alkaline Food Guide* will quickly become the resource you turn to at home, in restaurants, and whenever you want to select a food that can help you reach your health and dietary goals.

$7.95 • 208 pages • 4 x 7-inch mass paperback • ISBN 978-0-7570-0280-9

THE AMAZING ACID-ALKALINE COOKBOOK
Balancing Taste, Nutrition, and Your pH Levels
Bonnie Ross

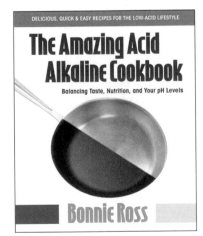

It's no secret that the foods we eat have a direct impact on our health. But did you know that for optimum wellness, the body needs the proper pH balance of acid and alkaline compounds, which are influenced by diet? The problem is that as a society, we tend to consume highly processed foods that produce acid. This makes us prone to a variety of health problems, from minor skin irritations to osteoporosis.

Bonnie Ross offers a solution with *The Amazing Acid-Alkaline Cookbook.* The book opens with pH basics, including an explanation of how an overly acidic body wreaks havoc on health. The author then presents ten chapters packed with over 140 kitchen-tested recipes for perfectly balanced dishes that are both satisfying and delicious. Choose from taste-tempting breakfast favorites, soups, salads, snacks, and sides, as well as delectable entrées, baked goods, and desserts.

With *The Amazing Acid-Alkaline Cookbook,* you'll learn how easy it is to make delicious meals that will naturally correct your body's pH balance, helping you regain vigor and well-being.

$17.95 • 176 pages • 7.5 x 9-inch quality paperback • ISBN 978-0-7570-0316-5

THE WORLD GOES RAW COOKBOOK
An International Collection of Raw Vegetarian Recipes
Lisa Mann

People everywhere know that meals prepared without heat can taste great and improve their overall health. Yet raw cuisine cookbooks have always offered little variety—until now. In *The World Goes Raw Cookbook,* raw food chef Lisa Mann provides a fresh approach to (un)cooking with recipes that have an international twist.

After discussing the healthfulness of a raw food diet, *The World Goes Raw Cookbook* tells you how to stock your kitchen with the tools and ingredients that make it easy to prepare raw meals. What follows are six recipe chapters, each focused on a different ethnic cuisine, including Italian, Mexican, Middle Eastern, Asian, Caribbean, and South American dishes. Whether you are already interested in raw food or are exploring it for the first time, the recipes in this book can add variety to your life while helping you feel healthy and energized.

$16.95 • 176 pages • 7.5 x 9-inch quality paperback • ISBN 978-0-7570-0320-2

EAT SMART, EAT RAW
Creative Vegetarian Recipes for a Healthier Life
Kate Wood

As the popularity of raw vegetarian cuisine continues to soar, so does the evidence that uncooked food is amazingly good for you. From lowering cholesterol to eliminating excess weight, the health benefits of this diet are too important to ignore. Now there is another reason to go raw—taste! In *Eat Smart, Eat Raw,* cook and health writer Kate Wood not only explains how to get started, but also provides kitchen-tested recipes guaranteed to delight even the fussiest of eaters.

Eat Smart, Eat Raw begins by discussing the basics of cooking without heat. This is followed by twelve chapters offering 150 recipes for truly exceptional dishes, including hearty breakfasts, savory soups, satisfying entrées, and luscious desserts. There's even a chapter on the "almost raw." Whether you are an ardent vegetarian or just someone in search of a great meal, *Eat Smart, Eat Raw* may forever change the way you look at an oven.

$15.95 • 184 pages • 7.5 x 9-inch quality paperback • ISBN 978-0-7570-0261-8

GOING WILD IN THE KITCHEN
The Fresh & Sassy Tastes of Vegetarian Cooking
Leslie Cerier

Go wild in the kitchen! Venture beyond the usual beans, grains, and vegetables to include an exciting variety of organic vegetarian fare in your meals. *Going Wild in the Kitchen* shows you how. In addition to providing helpful cooking tips and techniques, this book offers over 150 kitchen-tested recipes for taste-tempting dishes that contain such unique ingredients as edible flowers; tasty sea vegetables; wild mushrooms, berries, and herbs; and exotic ancient grains like teff, quinoa, and Chinese "forbidden" black rice. Author Leslie Cerier encourages the creative instincts of novice and seasoned cooks alike, prompting them to "go wild" by adding, changing, or substituting ingredients in existing recipes. Lively illustrations and a complete resource list for finding organic foods complete this user-friendly cookbook.

Going Wild in the Kitchen is more than a unique cookbook—it's a recipe for inspiration. Excite your palate with this treasure-trove of taste-tempting creations.

$16.95 • 240 pages • 7.5 x 9-inch quality paperback • ISBN 978-0-7570-0091-1

VICKI'S VEGAN KITCHEN
Eating with Sanity, Compassion & Taste
Vicki Chelf

Vegan dishes are healthy, delicious, and surprisingly easy to make. Yet many people are daunted by the idea of preparing meals that contain no animal products. For them, and for everyone who loves great food, vegetarian chef Vicki Chelf presents *Vicki's Vegan Kitchen,* a comprehensive cookbook designed to take the mystery out of meatless meals.

The book begins with an overview of the vegan diet, including its nutritional benefits and impact on weight control. Chapters on kitchen staples, cooking methods, and food preparation techniques come next, along with helpful shopping guidelines. Over 375 of Vicki's favorite recipes and recipe variations follow. Vicki shares delectable breakfast choices—from pancakes and waffles to hot cereals and scrambles—and shows you how to make heavenly breads, perfect pie crusts, and incredible homemade pasta. And every dish is a winner—easy to make and utterly delicious.

$17.95 • 320 pages • 7.5 x 9-inch quality paperback • ISBN 978-0-7570-0251-9

ENEMY OF THE STEAK
Vegetarian Recipes to Win Friends and Influence Meat-Eaters
Nikki and David Goldbeck

Don't blame vegetarians for starting this. Who said "real food for real people"? Aren't asparagus, carrots, and tomatoes every bit as real as . . . that other food? To answer the call to battle, Nikki and David Goldbeck have created a wonderfully tempting cookbook that offers a wealth of kitchen-tested recipes which nourish the body, please the palate, and satisfy even the heartiest of appetites.

Enemy of the Steak first presents basic information on vegetarian cooking. Then eight great chapters offer over 250 recipes for breakfast fare; appetizers and hors d'oeuvres; soups; salads; entrées; side dishes; sauces, toppings, and marinades; and desserts. A perfect marriage of nutrition and the art of cooking, *Enemy of the Steak* is for everyone who loves a good healthy meal. Simply put, it's great food for smart people. If you have to take sides, you couldn't be in better company.

$16.95 • 248 pages • 7.5 x 9-inch quality paperback • ISBN 978-0-7570-0273-1

GREENS AND GRAINS ON THE DEEP BLUE SEA COOKBOOK
Fabulous Vegetarian Cuisine from the Holistic Holiday at Sea Cruises
Sandy Pukel and Mark Hanna

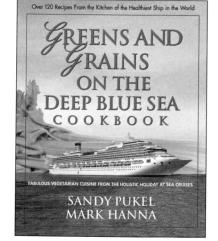

You are invited to come aboard one of America's premier health cruises. Too busy to get away? Even if you can't swim in the ship's pool, you can still enjoy its gourmet cuisine, because natural foods expert Sandy Pukel and master chef Mark Hanna have created *Greens and Grains on the Deep Blue Sea Cookbook*—a titanic collection of the most popular vegetarian dishes served aboard the Holistic Holiday at Sea cruises.

Each of the book's more than 120 recipes is designed to provide not only great taste, but also maximum nutrition. Choose from among an innovative selection of taste-tempting appetizers, soups, salads, entrées, side dishes, and desserts. Easy-to-follow instructions ensure that even novices will have superb results. With *Greens and Grains on the Deep Blue Sea Cookbook,* you can enjoy fabulous signature dishes from the Holistic Holiday at Sea cruises in the comfort of your own home.

$16.95 • 160 pages • 7.5 x 9-inch quality paperback • ISBN 978-0-7570-0287-8

For more information about our books,
visit our website at www.squareonepublishers.com